Exceptional Cars

The First Three Shelby Cobras

Porter Press International

Also published by Porter Press International

Ultimate Series
John Fitzpatrick Group C Porsches – The Definitive History
Works 956 Porsches – The Definitive History
McLaren F1 GTR – The Definitive History
Ferrari 250 GTO – The Definitive History

Great Cars Series
No. 1 – Jaguar Lightweight E-type – The autobiography of 4 WPD
No. 2 – Porsche 917 – The autobiography of 917-023
No. 3 – Jaguar D-type – The autobiography of XKD 504
No. 4 – Ferrari 250 GT SWB – The autobiography of 2119 GT
No. 5 – Maserati 250F – The autobiography of 2528
No. 6 – ERA – The autobiography of R4D
No. 7 – Ferrari 250 GTO – The autobiography of 4153 GT
No. 8 – Jaguar Lightweight E-type – The autobiography of 49 FXN
No. 9 – Jaguar C-type – The autobiography of XKC 051
No. 10 – Lotus 18 – The autobiography of Stirling Moss's '912'
No. 11 – Ford GT40 – The autobiography of 1075
No. 12 – Alfa Romeo Monza – The autobiography of the celebrated 2211130
No. 13 – Bugatti Type 50 – The autobiography of Bugatti's first Le Mans car
No.14 – Shelby Daytona Cobra – The autobiography of CSX2300

Exceptional Cars Series
No. 1 – Iso Bizzarrini – The remarkable history of A3/C 0222
No. 2 – Jaguar XK120 – The remarkable history of JWK 651
No. 3 – Ford GT40 MkII – The remarkable history of 1016
No. 4 – The First Three Shelby Cobras
No. 5 – Aston Martin Ulster – The remarkable history of CMC 614
No. 6 – Maserati 4CLT – The remarkable history of chassis no. 1600
No. 7 – Ferrari 250 LM – The remarkable history of 6313
No. 8 – Ferrari 250 GT SWB – The remarkable history of 2689
No. 9 – Ferrari 857S – The remarkable history of 0578M
No. 10 – Alfa Romeo T33/TT/3– The remarkable history of 115.72.002

Porter Profiles
No. 1 – Austin Healey – The story of DD 300
No. 2 – Jaguar D-type – The story of XKD 526

Bespoke books
The Le Mans Model Collection 1949-2009 (three-book set)
Derek Bell – All my Porsche races
DB4 G.T. Continuation – History in the making
One Formula, 50 years of car design – Gordon Murray
The Self Preservation Society – 50 Years of The Italian Job
The All-American Hero and Jaguar's Racing E-types
JUE 477 – The Remarkable History & Restoration of the World's First Production Land-Rover
ROFGO Collection
The Light Car Company Rocket
Ferrari 250 GTE
The Michael Turner Collection

Scrapbooks
Stirling Moss Scrapbook 1929-1954
Stirling Moss Scrapbook 1955
Stirling Moss Scrapbook 1956-1960
Stirling Moss Scrapbook 1961
Graham Hill Scrapbook 1929-1966
Murray Walker Scrapbook
Martin Brundle Scrapbook
Barry Cryer Comedy Scrapbook
Mini Scrapbook

The Jaguar Portfolio
Ultimate E-type – The Competition Cars
Jaguar E-type – The Definitive History (2nd edition)
Original Jaguar XK (3rd edition)
Jaguar Design – A Story of Style
Saving Jaguar

Deluxe leather-bound, signed, limited editions with slipcases are available for many titles. Books available from retailers or signed copies (of most titles) direct from the publishers. To order, simply phone +44 (0)1584 781588, visit the website or email sales@porterpress.co.uk

Keep up-to-date with news about current books and new releases at: **www.porterpress.co.uk**

Exceptional Cars

The First Three Shelby Cobras

The sports cars that changed the game

Gordon Bruce

Porter Press International

Dedicated to the memories of those All American Heroes – Carroll Shelby and Dan Gurney

© Porter Press International Ltd

All rights reserved. No part of this publication may be reproduced, stored in a retrieval system or transmitted, in any form or by any means, electronic, mechanical, photocopying, recording or otherwise, without prior permission in writing from the publisher

First published in February 2018
Reprinted in October 2020

978-1-907085-55-0

Published by
Porter Press International Ltd

Hilltop Farm, Knighton-on-Teme, Tenbury Wells, WR15 8LY, UK
Tel: +44 (0)1584 781588   Fax: +44 (0)1584 781630
sales@porterpress.co.uk
www.porterpress.co.uk

Edited by Ray Hutton
Design & Layout by Andrew Garman

Printed by Gomer Press Ltd

COPYRIGHT

We have made every effort to trace and acknowledge copyright holders and we apologise in advance for any unintentional omission. We would be pleased to insert the appropriate acknowledgement in any subsequent edition.

Contents

Introduction — 7

The first three Cobras — 8

1. Project Cobra — 10
2. Design and development — 24
3. Technical analysis — 34

CSX2000 — 44

4. The one and only prototype — 46

CSX2001 — 60

5. The first production Cobra — 62

CSX2002 — 88

6. The first works racing Cobra — 90

Epilogue — 114

7. Cobra later development — 116
8. The Shelby legacies — 124

Acknowledgements — 126
Index — 127

Introduction

While many of yesterday's sports cars have long since reversed into obscurity, the legend that is the Shelby Cobra seemingly knows no bounds. Posters of the Anglo-American masterpiece continue to adorn the walls of enthusiasts across the globe, while examples are still raced with vigour at the world's premier historic motor sport events. Even now, the alluring lines of this immortal snake turn the heads of the female of the species, just as they did in the 1960s – the seductive powers of this motor car are all-embracing!

Timing, they say, is everything and it was a sequence of unlikely coincidences that brought the Cobra into being. The rangy Texan Carroll Shelby had risen through the racing ranks to win Le Mans in 1959. Along the way he had grown to despise Ferrari and its founder; a sentiment that helped fuel his desire to create a car capable of beating the Prancing Horse in its own backyard. For many years the quintessentially British manufacturer AC Cars had enjoyed success with its Tojeiro-inspired Ace roadster, but now needed a meatier powerplant to give it a new lease of life. For its part in this three-legged saga, Ford Motor Company desperately required a model with which to challenge the all-conquering Corvette, both in the showroom and on the race track. Becoming the engine partner to Shelby's independent project suited the Blue Oval just fine – if things went well it could capitalise on the success but, if failure ensued, it could walk away relatively unscathed. Ever adept at spotting an opportunity, Shelby played both ends against the middle and persuaded AC to modify the ageing Ace to accept Ford's new thin-wall cast V8 engine, and cajoled the engine's maker into supporting the venture in return for having a weapon to temper Corvette sales that had been an increasing thorn in its side since 1953.

This absorbing backstory has been recounted many times – more often than not with varying degrees of fiction to enrich the already enticing facts, but there is no questioning that the Cobra had considerable impact on the world of road and racing sports cars on both sides of the Atlantic. This book is unique in primarily concerning itself with the first three Cobras made, namely the one and only prototype (CSX2000), the first production car (CSX2001) and the first works race car (CSX2002). All three vehicles nowadays dwell in the USA – CSX2000 and CSX2002 form part of the much-vaunted Larry Miller Collection of Shelby-inspired cars, while CSX2001 belongs to the internationally renowned private collector Bruce Meyer. It was on this trio that the incomparable Cobra phenomenon was founded.

Gordon Bruce
Buckinghamshire, England
February 2018

● The components of an automotive legend – Carroll Shelby and the one and only Cobra prototype CSX2000.
Private collection

Part 1
The first three Cobras

CSX2000 caused quite a stir when it was unleashed to the American press in spring 1962 – although based on an already antiquated chassis, it combined breathtaking bodywork with an astounding level of performance. Since those heady days, many a chancer has claimed ownership of a Cobra prototype but, as all aficionados of the model know, there was only ever the one pre-production example, which caused a second media storm in 2016 when it sold at auction for a cool $13.75 million.

CSX2001 was another landmark Cobra – it was not only the first production version, but the first to be assembled by Shelby's East Coast distributor, European Cars Inc. of Pittsburgh, Pennsylvania, and the first to dip a wheel into the world of competition. Although bred in the United States, it was in Europe that CSX2001 really made its mark, appearing in such major events as the Le Mans Test Weekend and the Tour de France Automobile in 1964 before posting significant results in hill-climbs.

CSX2002 was built to lead the charge on the circuits. It would have achieved an historic inaugural victory at the Riverside Raceway, California in October 1962 in the hands of Bill Krause, but for the inopportune breakage of a rear hub. The first win came four months later, courtesy of Dave MacDonald, and the car was subsequently piloted by Dan Gurney and Ken Miles before beginning a new career in Canada, where it whisked Eppie Wietzes and then Jean Ouellet to numerous triumphs.

● The first three Shelby Cobras are automotive celebrities these days, and in regular demand for key events around the world. Here the first two sit side by side at the 2012 Pebble Beach Concours d'Elegance.
Private collection

Chapter 1
Project Cobra

A natural entrepreneur, Carroll Shelby was prepared to turn his hand to anything, but had yet to fully make his mark on the world until his innate ability behind the wheel of a racing car drew the attention of Aston Martin's John Wyer. It was Wyer who placed him firmly on the international stage, which ultimately led to his famous victory with Roy Salvadori at Le Mans in 1959. Much as he had loved, and excelled in, the domestic American racing scene, his time on the best of the European circuits not only left him yearning for more international success, but recognition courtesy of a car of his own rather than somebody else's creation.

When heart problems forced Shelby's premature retirement from the circuits at the end of the 1960 season, the desire grew ever stronger. However, he possessed relatively little engineering knowledge and no money, so creating a Ferrari challenger from scratch was out of the question – he was also a man in a hurry and therefore in search of a quick automotive fix.

Having successfully raced an Allard J2X early in his career, Shelby was aware of the potential advantages of teaming a lightweight British-designed and built sports car with American V8 muscle. With this in mind, he is reputed to have approached Healey, Aston Martin and other manufacturers with his plan, but without success.

The AC Ace was another British product with which he was more than familiar, owing to the model's considerable success in American sports car racing, and when he contacted its maker in the autumn of 1961 it transpired he was pushing an open door. Bristol's BMW-inspired 2-litre engine had been the preferred option of Ace customers since 1956, but the car's latest rivals were more powerful. More pertinently, as Bristol had just moved over to large-capacity American V8s for its own model range, the production days of the 2-litre engine were numbered. Thanks to the suggestion of renowned AC racer and car tuner Ken Rudd, AC had begun offering the Ace with the 2.6 litre straight-six unit of the MkII Ford Zephyr, but didn't see it as a long-term solution and thus broadly agreed to Shelby's proposal, providing a suitable American engine could be sourced.

Shelby initially approached General Motors, but of course it already had a performance sports car, the Corvette, and did not feel the need of another. The story was very different at Ford, who had created a new thin-wall lightweight 221cu.in. (3.6-litre) V8 for the Fairlane that seemed ideal for the type of multi-role car Shelby envisaged. Moreover, Ford was not only desperate to supply its dealers with a rival for the Corvette, but also to add a roadgoing race car to its upcoming Total Performance programme – the none-too-subtle shift in image from safety to performance by which it planned to attract America's car-crazy baby boomers.

Shelby's dream was suddenly on the road to reality and Ford stuck a toe in his pond by delivering one of the new engines to AC Cars at the beginning of November 1961. The engine's arrival reputedly flummoxed the company's storeman, who had no idea what was in the crate, but imagined its strange foreign-looking FoMoCo label meant it probably hailed from Japan – FoMoCo is of course nothing more bizarre than a contraction of Ford Motor Company!

What's in a name? One of the oft quoted items of Shelby folklore is that the Cobra moniker came to

This company publicity shot of an early 289 model serves as a reminder of how visually similar the first Cobras were to the last of the Aces, the wheelarch extensions being the only major difference. Giles Chapman collection

Project Cobra

● AC Ace BEX 229 at the 1958 Sebring 12 Hours, where it was a class winner in the hands of George McClure, Duncan Forlong and Richard Milo, later the first owner of Cobra CSX2001.
David Milo

● This image displays AC Ace chassis AE01 – the first production example of the model. When compared with the later Ace 2.6 and Cobra, note the flatter windscreen and Ferrari-esque styling around the radiator grille.
Giles Chapman collection

Carroll in a dream, by which he was awoken sufficiently to jot the word down on a notepad retained by his bed for just such eventualities. The veracity of the detail is by now immaterial, as the label proved to be a truly inspired choice and continues to spawn a range of eye-catching reptilian headlines, while setting the pulses of enthusiasts racing with expectation. The Cobra name even encouraged Alejandro de Tomaso to select Mangusta for the name of his Giugiaro-penned successor to the Vallelunga, as Mangusta is Italian for mongoose – a creature renowned for its ability to fight and kill venomous snakes, especially cobras!

Work on Shelby's prototype began in mid-November 1961 and almost exactly three months later the finished car was despatched to Shelby American's temporary home in Santa Fe Springs, California, that consisted of no more than a small corner of the premises belonging to renowned hot-rodder Dean Moon. It had been an astonishing turnaround, though probably seemed

● The Cobra was based on the AC Ace 2.6, not the Ace Bristol, and already featured many of the chassis and body updates often erroneously attributed to the Cobra – such as the low bonnet line and narrower, slanting intake. *Giles Chapman collection*

like a lifetime to Shelby himself, who was desperate to get the programme underway and cement his tacit arrangement with Ford. Until the first cars rolled out of the door there would be no income and that was a potential problem for the impecunious Shelby.

Enter Ed Hugus, a regular racer on the American national circuit who also competed at Le Mans for no fewer than 10 consecutive years. A friend of Shelby's, Hugus was appointed: American Cobra distributor for all states east of the Mississippi; the first dealer; and the first assembler, as which his European Cars organisation would ultimately put together some 19 early examples, starting with CSX2001. More fundamentally, according to a recent biography on the man, Hugus funded the first seven cars out of his own pocket – an act of trust and generosity without which it seems the project might not have lasted long enough for Ford to commit to a fully financed agreement.

'The Cobra name even encouraged Alejandro de Tomaso to select Mangusta for the name of his Giugiaro-penned successor to the Vallelunga.'

Project Cobra

- The Cobra's home-grown competition was the Chevrolet Corvette, in the showroom and on American circuits.
Giles Chapman collection

- The Ferrari 250 GT SWB, seen here on the 1961 Tour de France, was the GT star on the world racing stage when the Cobra came along.
The Revs Institute for Automotive Research/ George Phillips

- Just hours from hitting the streets for the first time, the one and only Cobra prototype CSX2000 is rapidly taking shape in a corner of hot-rodder Dean Moon's garage in Santa Fe Springs, California.
The Henry Ford/Dave Friedman

Project Cobra

An early publicity shot of CSX2000 taken at the Riverside Raceway, where the car would later do service at the Carroll Shelby School of Racing. The helmet is Peter Brock's. The identity of the lady is unknown.
Private collection

Clarification

The Cobra story has been recounted many times to the point where, 55 years on, it is ever harder to distinguish some of the so-called facts from fiction. However, as we are primarily concerned here with the first three examples made, it is fundamental to confirm the correct serial numbers for these cars, as they have frequently been misquoted over the years.

CSX

The AC-derived prefix is sometimes interpreted as '**C**arroll **S**helby e**X**perimental'. In fact, it stood for the slightly less exciting '**C**arroll **S**helby e**X**port'. The related prefixes were: **COB** – **CO**bra **B**ritain (right-hand drive cars for sale in Great Britain) and **COX** – **CO**bra e**X**port (left-hand drive cars for export to countries other than Great Britain and the USA).

2000/2001/2002

The serial number attributed to the prototype has sometimes been incorrectly quoted as CSX0001. In fact, Shelby leaf spring roadster serial numbers were all four digit ones beginning with '2' and starting with 2000, making the first three cars CSX2000, CSX2001 and CSX2002.

Ford Motor Company

● Henry Ford II invested a vast sum of the Blue Oval's money in initiating his Total Performance programme. By the time the Cobra was in full production, Shelby was assured of Ford's backing and the 'Powered by Ford' message became a discreet badge on all Cobra flanks.
Getty Images/Bettmann

Although the mighty Blue Oval needs no introduction, it is important to understand why a generally confident and self-sufficient company was prepared to temporarily hang its competition hat on an almost penniless, failed chicken farmer.

At the time Shelby knocked on his corporate door, Henry Ford II was busy rebuilding his company's motor sport strategy after years of non-participation, which had resulted from a voluntary agreement between Ford and the other members of the American Automobile Manufacturers' Association. The company's so-called Total Performance programme was intended to embrace competition on both sides of the Atlantic and at both national and international level. The problem in terms of the all-important sports car segment was plain for all to see: Ford did not have one, a situation that had been a bone of contention for the dealers for many years.

On that basis, Ford had little to lose from at least exploring a union with Shelby, and much to gain if things went well. History shows that while the Cobra was not a financial success for any of those involved, it did finally give enthusiasts a reason to visit Ford showrooms and greatly raised the company's profile with the general public, to whom it needed to sell its other products.

The union was in full swing when Ford's attempts to buy Ferrari failed and Henry Ford made it very plain he planned to make *Il Commendatore* pay for the failure of the talks that had originally looked so promising – by which he meant beating Ferrari not just in the US, but in its native Europe. When even the talents of former Aston Martin team manager John Wyer failed to make the GT40 work in 1964, who else would Ford approach to save the day but that man Shelby?

Success was slow to come in 1965, but 1966 produced that treasured first Le Mans win, with a further victory in 1967, this time with American drivers at the helm. Shelby was also tasked with making the Mustang a winner on both road and track until Shelby American and the Ford Motor Company temporarily fell out of love – by which time the unlikely marriage had proved its worth several times over.

AC Cars

The history of AC Cars is a tangled web, from which has spun items as diverse as the 'Bag Boy' (an all-alloy, independently sprung golf trolley), trains for the seaside pier of English coastal town Southend, and invalid carriages constructed for the UK's Ministry of Health. Incredibly, this is the same AC that provided the basis for the Cobra.

The story began in 1904 when Autocars & Accessories was founded by butcher John Portwine and engineer John Weller for the purpose of building a wooden-framed three-wheeled delivery vehicle, the Auto-Carrier. It caught on, encouraging the creation of a passenger version, the Sociable. A four-wheeled Fivet-engined lightcar then ensued, but few were made before the intervention of the First World War.

Immediately following hostilities, Weller unveiled his six-cylinder overhead camshaft engine that was to remain in production for a record-breaking 44 years. In 1921, former works Napier driver SF Edge assumed control of what was soon to be renamed AC Cars and instituted a programme of racing and record-breaking. This led to JA Joyce's victories in the 1923 and 1924 Brighton Speed Trials, and the Hon. Victor Bruce's win in the 1926 Monte Carlo Rally – the first for a British car. Despite numerous such successes, the depression took its toll, the receiver was summoned and the remains of the company were sold to successful hauliers William and Charles Hurlock. This sparked a golden period during which a memorable line of lean, low saloons, drop-head coupés and tourers was produced.

The post-World War II 2 Litre models were less remarkable, but next door to where the Buckland four-seater tourer versions were bodied worked one John Tojeiro, a talented young racing car designer of Portuguese extraction. He was busy turning out class-winning two-seater sports cars based on a simple lightweight ladder frame, complete with all-round independent suspension. Engine and body choice were left to the purchaser.

Enamoured of the Ferrari 166 Barchetta-styled example built for Tojeiro's landlord Vin Davison, Buckland boss Ernie Bailey suggested it should be shown to AC, which was now being managed by Charles Hurlock and William Hurlock's son Derek. It was an astute move – they purchased the car there and then, agreed a deal with Tojeiro to employ the design as the basis for their new sports car, and even hired Davison to help them develop it. Just three months later, the new AC Ace was the toast of the 1953 London Motor Show and the family tree that culminated in the Cobra had been planted. Aces raced with distinction on both sides of the Atlantic and in three Le Mans outings finished 10th (1957), eighth (1958) and seventh (1959). The last placing was good enough for a class win, a result that may very well have been noted for future reference by that year's outright winner – one Carroll Shelby.

AC largely ceased manufacture of the Ace once Cobra production was fully up and running. While most examples of the newcomer were reserved for the USA, the company did go on to sell AC-branded versions of the leaf spring model, plus the ensuing AC 289 (effectively a coil spring Cobra with a 289 instead of the 427 engine) in the UK and Europe. Then, spotting the potential for a grand touring Cobra, AC commissioned Italian stylist Pietro Frua to design a suitable body for a lengthened version of the chassis. Some 80 examples of the AC 428 were built between 1965 and 1973.

A recession, the protracted birth of the mid-engined 3000ME, and ill-health, conspired to bring the Hurlock era to a close after 56 years, at which point ownership passed to a partnership of Autokraft and Ford, with Autokraft's Brian Angliss assuming full control in 1992. Fresh evolutions of the Cobra and an all-new Ace resulted, but by 1996 AC was again in financial trouble, at which point it was acquired by South African Alan Lubinsky, who retains the rights to this day.

Before and after the Cobra. In the top picture, Vin Davison stands proudly beside his Tojeiro that became the prototype AC Ace and, right, the AC 428, developed in the UK as a grand touring version of the Cobra.
Private Collection

Carroll Hall Shelby

● No wonder the man is smiling, his dream is fast becoming reality as Dean Moon's band of happy hot-rodders assemble the prototype Cobra around him. Within no time he was out on the streets of Santa Fe Springs seeking Corvettes to bait!
The Henry Ford/Dave Friedman

There was little about Shelby's rural American childhood that marked him out as a global automotive phenomenon, though petrol was certainly detected in his veins at an early age. He entered the world via the backwater Texan town of Leesburg in November 1923.

Shelby Senior was the local postman whose round was conducted on horseback for the first four years of Carroll's life, but in 1927 he graduated to a two-years-old Overland family saloon and Carroll's life-long love affair with the motor car was under way. It was further fuelled by visits to the Dallas 'bull rings' – oval dirt tracks where the motor racing was fast and furious.

Carroll not only yearned to be a racing driver, but an aviator too and spent the war in the United States Army Air Corps as a flight instructor and test pilot. As matters transpired, he was never required to venture beyond the Gulf of Mexico, but was nevertheless forced to cope with both a wheels-up landing following the loss of both engines and a fiery bail-out – both of which incidents occurred aboard twin-engined Beechcraft AT-11s.

Once demobbed, he became embroiled in the trucking world with his best friend from schooldays. They hauled gravel, ready-mix concrete and timber, but struggled to make ends meet. He then spent six months as a roughneck in the oil fields before embarking on his more famous venture as a chicken farmer. The first batch of broilers reputedly netted him some $5,000 and the future looked bright. However, the second batch of 80,000 birds died of disease and left him bankrupt.

It was while Shelby was deciding how next to put food on the family table that he finally became involved in motor sport. His first competitive turn at the wheel, and victory, occurred in January 1952, and was in a quarter-mile drag event at the wheel of 'The Monster', a friend's flat-head Ford V8-powered hot-rod. His first proper circuit drives, and wins, followed four months later, courtesy of the same friend's MG TC.

In these health and safety controlled days it is hard to imagine the era when drivers raced in whatever they found most comfortable. Whilst a chicken farmer, Carroll had worn Carhartt striped bib overalls and continued to do so when doing chores at home. On a hot August day in 1953 he was still wearing them when he arrived at Eagle Mountain National Guard

Airbase, Fort Worth, to race an Allard J2X. His rivals initially ribbed him mercilessly, but less so after he had 'whooped their asses'. The clothing became a Shelby trademark, along with his Stetson hat and leather belt.

Carroll's international racing break came in January 1954. The Sports Car Club of America (SCCA) had been invited to field a team of US drivers at the opening round of the World Sports Car Championship in Buenos Aires, and the club elected to field Masten Gregory (Jaguar C-Type), Phil Hill (Ferrari 340 Mexico), Bob Said (OSCA MT4) and Carroll Shelby (Allard J2X). The Allard caught fire, suffered several burst tyres and was literally falling apart by the end, yet Shelby and co-driver Dale Duncan finished 10th among the works entries of Ferrari, Maserati and Aston Martin, whose team manager John Wyer was impressed by the Texan's spirited driving.

In August 1954, Shelby was a key part of the Austin-Healey team that broke 83 international and national records at the Bonneville salt flats. This created a relationship with English former World War II RAF pilot Roy Jackson-Moore that led to them sharing a Healey 100S on the Carrera Panamericana. Remembered Jackson-Moore: 'We competed together on the first day but hated each other's driving. I was therefore allowed to fly ahead on day two, and it's just as well I did, as Carroll had a massive accident. Had I been in the passenger seat I would not have survived.' Shelby was certainly alive but had badly fractured his right olecranon, commonly known as the 'funny bone'. This was no laughing matter for the tough Texan, whose prime concern was when he could get back behind the wheel. The answer was three months later, and even then his arm was in a glass-fibre cast that had to be taped to the steering wheel. This was a man with a burning mission, and it was going to take a lot more than a smashed limb to slow him down.

By 1956 Shelby was back in full swing, mainly piloting privately entered Ferraris on the American domestic scene. This netted him *Sports Illustrated* magazine's 'Driver of the Year' award, a feat he repeated the following season. By now he was a big name among US enthusiasts and in 1957 he founded Carroll Shelby Sport Cars in Dallas, from which you could purchase anything from a Morris Minor to a Maserati. With little left to prove in his native country, he then opted to spend most of 1958 and 1959 racing in Europe, driving privately entered F1 Maseratis and works F1 cars and sports cars for Aston Martin. His best F1 result in eight starts was fourth in the 1958 Italian Grand Prix aboard a Maserati 250F. However, the pinnacle of his impressive racing career was without doubt his victory with Roy Salvadori in the 1959 24 Hours of Le Mans.

What most people were unaware of was that, having apparently outgrown a heart condition that affected his early childhood, he was now sometimes in real pain and only finishing races courtesy of nitroglycerin pills. After

Shelby and his wife Jeanne together with the Roy Cherryholmes Allard that kick-started Carroll's racing career. After multiple wins on home territory, Shelby and the Allard drew the attention of Aston Martin's John Wyer in Argentina. *Private collection*

Project Cobra

Shelby parked proudly outside the Carroll Shelby Sport Cars emporium he founded in Dallas in 1957. Reputedly, it could supply anything from a Morris Minor to a Maserati.
Private collection

earlier misdiagnoses, in May 1960 it was concluded he was suffering from angina pectoris. He was also tired of living out of suitcases and his marriage had hit the buffers, so he decided to hang up his helmet at the end of the season. Being Shelby, he did not depart with a whimper but as the newly-crowned USAC champion. The good news was he could now focus on his long-held dream of becoming a car manufacturer. The bad news was he was back needing a means of putting food on the table. This prompted the foundation of the Carroll Shelby School of Racing and then contracts for the distribution of both Goodyear tyres and Champion spark plugs.

Of course his sports car (or 'sport' car, as he insisted on calling it) dream eventually morphed into the mighty Cobra, which led to him helping Ford win Le Mans with the GT40 and to develop the iconic Shelby version of the Mustang, and later fathering projects for Dodge. Against the odds, this perennially colourful Texan survived to the ripe old age of 89, leaving a legacy that continues to fire the passions of 'sport' car enthusiasts the world over.

The pinnacle of Shelby's short but remarkable race driving career was unquestionably his victory in the 1959 Le Mans 24 Hours, with Englishman Roy Salvadori in a works Aston Martin DBR1.
Getty Images

Carroll Shelby in a Birdcage Maserati at Riverside in 1960 – his final season before heart problems put an end to his driving career. His preferred number of 98 was later adopted by Cobra legend Ken Miles.
Private collection

In 1966 a Shelby American GT40 MkII achieved the first of four Ford wins at Le Mans. Shelby could eventually lay claim to conquering the race as a driver (1959), constructor (1964) and team manager (1966).
Sutton Images

Chapter 2
Design and development

The typical path to the production of a new car by a small volume manufacturer back in the 1960s would have been to perfect the design on a drawing board and then create a rough prototype to test the thinking. Once the major bugs had been ironed out, further prototypes would ensue, until the company felt ready to take its newcomer to market.

This was not the story of the Cobra, for several reasons. Most fundamentally, although Shelby American was a new company and the model a potential game-changer in the global sports car market, in technical terms it was the development of an existing vehicle rather than an all-new design. Also, the burning motivation behind it was the creation of a production sports car that would beat Ferrari on the global racing stage – selling cars to the public was therefore a necessary (though not unwelcome) adjunct to that goal, rather than the prime focus. Under the circumstances, perfecting his new toy for road use was of secondary concern to Shelby, who was impatient to get it on track where, from his point of view, the most relevant development would take place.

An oft-portrayed impression is that, come 1961, the days of AC Cars were numbered and the company was only saved from imminent extinction by Carroll Shelby jetting across the Atlantic and persuading its management to play a key role in his embryo sports car plans. This is a somewhat distorted view. As is the equally frequently-presented premise that almost everything about the venerable AC Ace that formed the basis of the resulting Cobra had to be either redesigned or substantially modified. As this book will demonstrate, despite the mere three months involved in the design and production of the prototype, AC's talented team did such a masterly job of mating the American supplied powerplant and gearbox with its proven British chassis, that surprisingly little of the recently created 2.6-litre Ford-engined version needed upgrading. That revision of some components was required once the newcomer was subjected to the rigours of racing is hardly a surprise, as the engine output was now some 160 per cent higher than the chassis was originally required to cope with, and was set to climb further still in the coming years.

Chronicling the tiny differences between the first three Cobras 55 years after their creation is a nigh on impossible task, as development in a company like Shelby American is a by-the-minute phenomenon. However, the fact that there were only five days between the shipping of CSX2001 to Pennsylvania and CSX2002 to California suggests there would have been few differences in their pre-delivery specification – certainly nothing fundamental enough to be recorded by the Shelby World Registry. Of more significance is to consider the differences between them and the prototype – CSX2000.

The most obvious one is that CSX2000 was the only Cobra ever to feature inboard rear brakes. Period comment suggests Shelby went that route to minimise unsprung weight, or maybe the thinking was inspired by the Jaguar E-type that featured such a set-up in conjunction with exactly the same Salisbury differential. AC Cars was never in favour of the idea and by the time of the first production Cobra, CSX2001,

Worth many millions of dollars in today's market, a row of Cobras dominates the scene outside the famous Shelby American works at 1042 Princeton Drive, Venice Beach, California – now part of Marina del Rey.
The Henry Ford/Dave Friedman

Design and development

the switch to outboard rear discs had been made amid concern over potential cooling problems and the practicality of servicing discs and pads in the heat of competition. By comparison, the other tweaks were just detail alterations that included: moving the fuel tank from the boot floor to behind the rear bulkhead, and the filler cap from the nearside to the centre of the rear bodywork; replacing the Ace boot-lid with a shorter version and the squat Ace over-riders with beefier examples, and axing the full boot trim.

The fact is the more discernible changes came after CSX2001 and CSX2002 were in service. For example:

- Replacement of the 260cu.in. engine with the 289cu.in. engine (from CSX2075 onwards).
- Switch from worm-and-sector steering to rack-and-pinion (from CSX2126 onwards), with which came revised front suspension geometry, cast rather than fabricated uprights, and a dished rather than flat steering wheel.

● The first Cobras were fitted with the 260cu.in. V8 Ford engine. It was replaced early in the production sequence by the 289. Note that at this stage the prototype is still wearing an AC badge – Shelby ensured it was removed before the car's first public appearance.
The Henry Ford/Dave Friedman

26 | Exceptional Cars

Phil Remington

Shelby was fortunate to win Phil Remington in the deal to acquire the Venice Beach premises of Lance Reventlow's Scarab operation. A naturally gifted engineer, 'Rem' was key to the development of the Cobra and the MkII and MkIV derivations of the GT40.
The Revs Institute for Automotive Research/ Jean Charles Martha

Shelby, generally an arch self-promoter, was nevertheless unequivocal in his respect for Remington: 'Rem was the single reason the Cobras and GT40s were as successful as they were. I couldn't have done anything without Phil Remington.' Dan Gurney is on record as saying: 'He was a marvel, an old salt, and an inspiration to young and old.'

Remington was still working full-time a year before he passed away in 2013 at the grand old age of 92. A native Californian, his distinguished engineering career began as a component inspector for Northrop Aircraft. Come World War II and keen to follow his friends into the Army Air Corps, he not only lied about his age but avoided discovery of his colour blindness by memorising the test charts, and so lived out the war as a B-24 flight engineer in the South Pacific. Already a proven petrolhead, he would have gone on to race, but a severe motorcycle accident that hospitalised him for a year, and almost cost him a leg, caused him to turn to fabricating and fettling competition cars rather than driving them.

He initially worked with friends building everything from engine conversion kits to complete vehicles, and even developing parts for hydroplanes, before being appointed chief engineer for Lance Reventlow's high-profile Scarab racing car projects. It was the eventual failure of that business that in June 1962 allowed Shelby to adopt the company's premises at 1042 Princeton Drive, Venice Beach, Los Angeles, complete with Phil Remington.

Generally trusting, but determined to ensure things were done the way Remington knew they should be, caused him to take over from others at times – a trait that prompted Shelby competition administrator Al Dowd to nickname him STP, or 'Super Twitchy Phil'. Though modest to the last, he was not unaware of his value to Shelby American, and reputedly signed off his engineering blueprints with 'Draftsman: Remington', 'Designer: Remington', 'Engineer: Remington', 'Approved by: Remington'.

Having been key to the development of the Cobra in all its forms as well as the MkII and MkIV derivations of the GT40, Remington remained with Shelby until 1968, when he had a season overseeing Holman & Moody's stock car programme. But the change didn't suit him and he returned to California in a senior position with Dan Gurney's All American Racers (AAR), where he remained for a staggering 40-plus years.

We will leave the last word to Dan Gurney:

'In the heady, tumultuous, political atmosphere of Shelby American, Phil Remington was a man left alone to do it his way. Carroll did not pester him because he knew that Rem would be able to solve almost any problem that arose from the new Cobra venture. When others scratched their heads and tried to pinpoint a technical problem, Phil was already banging out parts that were finished masterpieces.

'He was a teacher and mentor to a team of young fabricators who came to worship the ground he walked on. He was not subtle with his comments but blunt and forthright; the team listened because they knew they were learning from the best.

'Phil's courage, resilience and know-how would get the job done. His contribution to the success of the Cobra and the Shelby mystique cannot be rated highly enough.'

Design and development

- Change from 5.5in. to 6in. wire wheels and the fitment of vents to the rear of the front wings to help reduce temperature levels within the engine compartment and prevent the battery from overheating (from CSX2160 onwards).
- Replacement of the original Delaney-Gallay radiator with (as a somewhat desperate stop-gap) a Harrison alloy unit purchased from GM dealers, followed by a Ford McCord product to help overcome ongoing cooling problems.
- Replacement of the original, rather amateurish nose badge with the first so-called 'Flat Head' emblem from CSX2031, and then the final version from CSX2133 onwards.

In reality, the development process never finished, and every time issues on the track required a tweak from the hand of master developer Phil Remington, the solution was immediately fed back to the production line – starting with the modification of the rear hubs that cost the Cobra victory at its first official race.

One can all too easily imagine the frustration of any unreliability in the early days of Cobra competition.

● It is not hard to imagine the excitement as the assembly of the first Cobra, CSX2000, neared completion in Dean Moon's workshop. Here the car is clearly almost ready to strut its stuff.
The Henry Ford/Dave Friedman

Unlike 99 per cent of the production models, CSX2000 was delivered unpainted and Moon's staff reputedly used a whole box of Brillo pads readying the alloy body for its first viewing by the media. ●
The Henry Ford/Dave Friedman

Design and development

Ken Miles

- The specials built and raced by Englishman Ken Miles had earned him a place in SCCA folklore before Shelby hired him to help develop the Cobra. His contribution to that programme is inestimable, and his death at the wheel of the Ford J-2 especially sad.
Private collection

Englishman Ken 'Teddy Teabag' Miles (so christened by his colleagues because of his love of Britain's favourite beverage) had raced motorcycles before serving as a tank sergeant in World War II. Following the war, he graduated to four wheels and campaigned a Ford V8-engined Frazer Nash and variety of other cars in Vintage Sports Car Club events before emigrating to California early in 1952.

A talented self-taught engineer and fast, mechanically sympathetic driver, Miles was soon cleaning up in US national events, and his MG-based 'Flying Shingle' and Porsche-engined Cooper dubbed 'Pooper' are enshrined in SCCA folklore. He was racing a relatively lowly Sunbeam Alpine when Shelby came knocking. Carroll figured he was the right man to help develop his Cobra, and history confirms it was the combined skills of Miles and Remington that turned what started as an AC Ace with Ford V8 engine into an all-conquering sports car in its own right.

With Miles, Shelby effectively obtained two first class men for the price of one, for when he wasn't developing the Cobra during the week he was taking one or another to victory at the weekend. At times his race leads were so long as to be embarrassing and, having lapped the leading Corvettes in a 1963 race at Riverside Raceway, he reputedly pitted for a drink of water in order to give them a chance to catch up, and then returned to the track in time to lap them all over again.

Nowadays we rely on computer programmes to improve handling and reduce lap times. In the 1960s it was largely down to the man behind the wheel, and it was Miles's ability to drive a car on and beyond the limit, and know what would further improve it, that made him so invaluable to Shelby American for the Cobra and ensuing programmes. When the 289cu.in. Cobra could no longer be guaranteed to outrun the opposition, he created the one and only pre-production 427cu.in.prototype by shoehorning a big-block engine (initially, a 427 but ultimately a special alloy-block 390cu.in. version of the Ford FE unit) into the nose of the unsuspecting Cobra 289 CSX2196. Displaying an equivalent level of innovation to Miles's early specials, it ultimately featured clamshell bodywork that opened akin to that of a GT40, which earned it the nickname of 'Flip-Top' Cobra; Miles less politely dubbed it 'The Turd'!

He also made a major contribution to the development of the Mustang GT350 and GT40, and should have become the first driver to win sports car racing's 'triple crown'. But, having triumphed in the 1966 Daytona and Sebring events, he was sadly cheated of victory at Le Mans by Ford's ill-judged attempt to engineer a dead-heat. Just two months later, one of the finest development/racing drivers of all time was dead – killed, aged 47, in a 200mph accident while testing the Ford J-2 car at Riverside Raceway.

Design and development

Shelby was desperate to put an end to Ferrari's dominance on the track – a company that had already won Le Mans six times. More fundamentally, Ford was playing a cautious hand and would have dropped the Cobra project like a ton of bricks had the company, at any stage, felt it was not of benefit to its aims or, worse still, harmful to its image. Of course, the alternative would have been to design and build a car from scratch, but as already explained this was never even a consideration due to Shelby's lack of funds and his desire to short-circuit the design and build phase. Even with hindsight, the birth and development of the Cobra was remarkably successful.

● This shot of CSX2000 under construction perfectly illustrates the miniature nature of a Cobra propshaft which, at around 10 inches long, is generally considered to be one of the shortest ever installed in a production car.
The Henry Ford/Dave Friedman

● There were three generations of Cobra badge. The first arguably amateur design was hurriedly commissioned by Shelby to replace the AC emblems of the early cars. Next came the so-called 'Flat Head' insignia that was then refined by Peter Brock into the version familiar to most Cobra enthusiasts.
Private collection

The First Three Shelby Cobras | 31

Design and development

Peter Brock

A young Peter Brock poses with the first Cobra Coupe, CSX2287. His colleagues and even an aviation expert said the design would never work. Brock stood his ground and had the last laugh – the first FIA World Championship victory ever achieved by an American car.
The Henry Ford/Dave Friedman

Brock had designs on being a professional racing driver, but ended up penning cars instead. It was during his first year of engineering studies at Stanford University, California, that he heard about the Art Center College of Design in Los Angeles where you could learn to be an automotive designer. He did not realise that it was a course for existing professionals and, when asked for his portfolio, had to admit he did not even know what the word meant. Undaunted, he returned to his car and spent two hours sketching hot rods in an old ring-binder. They must have been good, as he was promptly enrolled.

A fortuitous meeting with a General Motors headhunter led to Brock becoming the youngest (19-years-old) designer ever hired by the company's styling department. While there, he designed a stillborn students' car called the Cadet but, far more famously, created a sketch for a new Corvette that ultimately evolved into the immortal Sting Ray, the sports car that was to take the US market by storm some six years later.

By then he had tired of the corporate world and returned to his native California, complete with a Cooper-Climax, intent on rekindling his racing ambitions. He toiled on the car at night while working for Max Balchowsky's Hollywood Motors by day. Balchowsky was famous for his series of nine 'Old Yeller' racing cars, not to mention preparing and fettling the Mustangs and Dodge Chargers for the unsurpassed car chases of the Steve McQueen blockbuster *Bullitt*.

It was through Hollywood Motors that Brock met Carroll Shelby, who at the time was desperately seeking someone to run his racing school. Peter was standing in the right place at the right time and thus became Shelby's second employee (the first was Joan Cole, his PA, office manager and girlfriend, who was sometimes even described as the 'brains' behind Shelby American). Once Cobra production was up and running, Brock moved across to the manufacturing venture where he was variously responsible for the company's corporate identity, race car liveries and advertising.

Brock also designed the Lang Cooper, Nethercutt Mirage, De Tomaso P70 and, most famously, the Shelby Daytona Cobra Coupes that clinched the GT class of the 1965 World Sports Car Championship for Shelby and Ford. He left Shelby at the end of that year to form Brock Racing Enterprises (BRE), a business he these days runs with his wife Gayle. Its impressively diverse CV includes: creating and running winning race teams; building the world's biggest hang-gliding company and effectively transforming that sport; automotive photography and journalism; and creating a contemporary version of the Daytona Cobra Coupe that is marketed by Shelby International.

Design and development

'I created these'! Brock on the front row of the grid at the 2015 Goodwood Revival with two of the works Daytona Cobra Coupes – cars he had designed 52 years before.
Private collection

Chapter 3
Technical analysis

To the uninitiated, one Cobra is probably much like another – the purposeful overall shape is unmistakable. However, a leaf spring 260-engined example and coil spring 427-powered one are snakes of a completely different hue. This book is primarily concerned with the first three cars built, all of which featured leaf spring chassis and were equipped when new with Bishop worm-and-sector steering and the 260cu.in. version of Ford's Windsor small-block V8 engine.

CSX2000 has remained astonishingly original throughout its life, to the point of even retaining the fabricated exhaust manifolds hastily knocked together back in early 1962. As CSX2001 was raced almost from the get-go it was quick to receive the more powerful 289 engine, rack-and-pinion steering and other modifications as they became available. As the first works race car, CSX2002 was constantly uprated from its debut at the Riverside Raceway in October 1962, to the time it was sold to Ford of Canada late in the summer of 1963.

Body
The final iteration of the AC Ace was powered by the 2.6 litre straight-six Ford Zephyr engine, coincident with which the scuttle was subtly reshaped, the bonnet line lowered and the nose re-fashioned with a neater, forward-slanting intake containing a distinctive egg crate-style grille. So, most of the visual changes so often attributed to the Cobra had in fact preceded it – the most obvious exception is the light flaring of the wheel arches to take account of the Cobra's wider track; 2in. front and rear.

The construction of the bodywork was also carried over from the Ace. There were two main suppliers – the Bronlow Sheet Metal Company of Edgware and Shapecraft of Surbiton. The well-proven production process comprised wheeling small sections of 0.045in. thick aluminium that were then welded together on body bucks, of which each company retained a set - the total weight of the finished product was a mere 80lb. Once complete, the skins were delivered to the AC factory where they were lowered on to the chassis and riveted in place.

CSX2000 was delivered to the USA unpainted, but with the exception of some competition cars and a few other road versions, production leaf spring vehicles were painted before delivery. The standard choice was Red, White, Guardsman Blue, Princess Blue, Vineyard Green, Black, Maroon and Silver, of which Red was the most popular, accounting for some 19 percent of manufacture, including CSX2001 and CSX2002.

The early cars were all delivered on 5.5in. painted wire wheels. These were increased to 6in. from CSX2160, coincident with the introduction of engine bay vents towards the back of the front wings. Much of the brightwork was carried over from the Ace, as were its suitably curved and raked windscreen in order to improve the aerodynamics and reduce wind noise that would now be experienced at higher speeds.

The factory delivered CSX2000 with AC badges front a rear. However, in contravention of the agreement between the two companies, Shelby wasted no time in removing these and equipping the noses of the first 30 cars with a surprisingly crude oblong-shaped polished

Cobra 289 bodies were skilfully fabricated out of sections of 0.045in. thick aluminium and weighed just 80lb, including the bonnet and boot-lid. Once complete, the skins were riveted on to the chassis. *The Henry Ford/Dave Friedman*

Technical analysis

aluminium badge, on which a notably tiny AC logo was sandwiched between the words SHELBY and COBRA. By CSX2031 this had been superseded by the so-called 'Flat Head' Cobra emblem, which featured a snake image on a blue background and made no reference to AC at all. This was then refined and given a white background by Peter Brock and became the definitive emblem from CSX2133 onwards.

Chassis

The basics of the Cobra chassis can be traced back even further than many people realise and to the most unlikely source – the Fiat Topolino of the 1930s. The model's independent front suspension comprised a transverse leaf spring at the top and wishbones below, and it was the set-up from a crashed Topolino lying in the Cooper Car Company's yard in 1946 that John and Charles Cooper attached to the front of their prototype 500cc Formula 3 tubular ladder chassis. They then hit upon the idea of using another Fiat front end for the rear of their car, and so the general layout of Cooper's F3, F2 and even F1 cars was born. In 1953, engineer John Tojeiro revealed a Bristol-engined two-seater sports car along exactly the same principles. Forever known by its registration number LOY 500, it was clothed in a shapely alloy body containing more than a hint of the

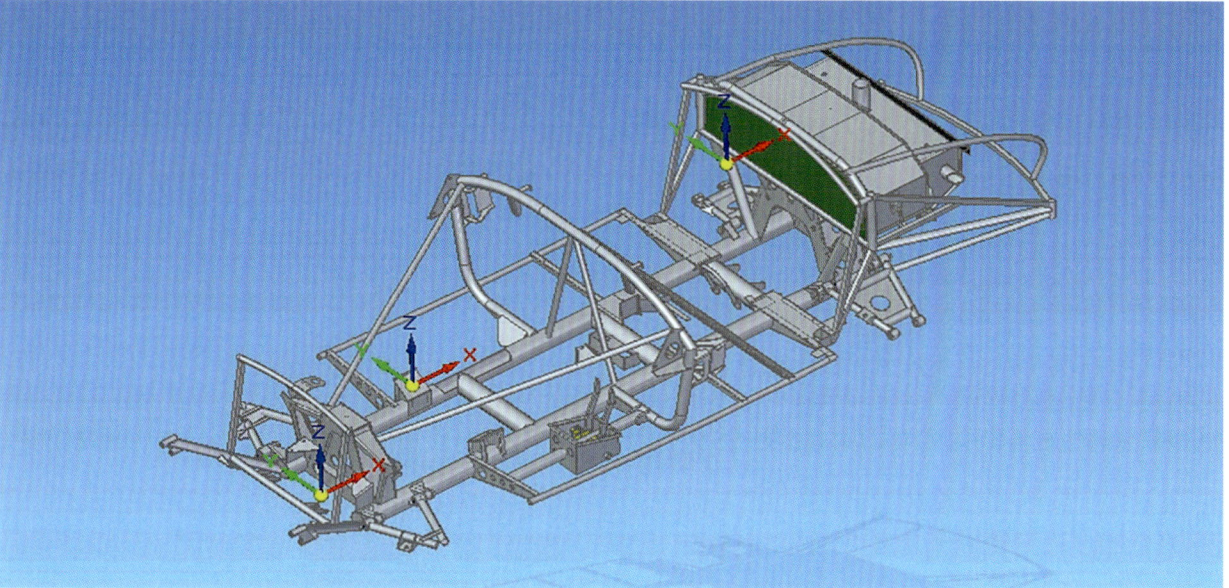

● Bare 289 chassis viewed from the front, in which the main tubes, suspension towers and superstructure are all clearly visible. On the left, a 289 Cobra chassis digitised by a state-of-the-art CAD design system; in this case that of North Devon Metalcraft who supply continuation body/chassis units to Shelby International.
North Devon Metalcraft

A rolling 289 Cobra chassis in which you ● can pick out the leaf spring and wishbone suspension, disc brakes, steering rack, glass-fibre foot boxes and fabricated battery tray.
North Devon Metalcraft

36 | Exceptional Cars

Technical analysis

- The interior of a Cobra is a unique mix of spartan sports car and luxury saloon. The dished wood-rim steering wheel denotes this as a rack-and-pinion car, and is in fact CSX2001 that had its steering system upgraded from worm-and-sector in period.
Peter Harholdt

contemporaneous Ferrari 166 Barchetta, and it was a replica of this on which AC based its Ace.

Shelby American did a good job of persuading the world that supplanting the straight-six AC (100bhp), Bristol (125bhp) and Ford (up to 170bhp) engines of the Ace with the original Ford 260bhp V8 unit of the Cobra required a very considerable degree of reworking of the old Tojeiro-designed chassis. It did not, and the only major differences between the frames of the later Aces and early Cobras were limited to an increase in the wall thickness of the main 3in. chassis tubes from 14 to 13SWG, and the general beefing up of the rear end in order to replace the trusty ENV differential with the more robust Salisbury 4HU unit, as used in the Jaguar Mk X and E-type. To take account of the extra weight of the Salisbury and the considerably greater torque of the V8 engine, the rear suspension tower was completely redesigned and a cross-member added to support the nose of the differential casing.

Thanks to Ford's new thin-wall casting technique, the weight of the Cobra engine was in fact lighter than the ones ultimately used to drive the Ace. Obviously new mountings were required and the opportunity was taken to keep the new powerplant well back in the frame, all of which resulted in an almost perfect front/rear weight distribution of 48/52. The superstructure - a lightweight network of round and square tubes – was primarily the same as that employed for the Ace 2.6, to which the alloy Cobra body was riveted in exactly the same way.

Interior

Also very much a carry-over from the Ace, the cockpit of a standard production Cobra is a unique mix of spartan sports car and luxury saloon. The overall layout of the interior changed very little from the birth of the prototype CSX2000 to the end of the model's programme in 1967.

There are no exterior door handles, entry being gained by the operation of a simple leather cord attached to the inside door latch. The weather equipment comprises a pair of clip-on sidescreens with sliding panes and the choice of tonneau cover or rudimentary soft top, all of which need to be left at home or squeezed into the boot when not required. The occupants are ensconced in a pair of leather-trimmed semi-bucket seats – supportive by road standards, but generally replaced by lighter, more figure-hugging examples by those taking to the track. Carpet adorns the floor and door cards.

Dominating the view below the wrap-around windscreen is the large, lightly canted facia. Ahead of the driver are speedometer and rev-counter. To their right are three descending rows of auxiliary gauges comprising: ammeter, water temperature and oil temperature; fuel and oil pressure; and a clock. Around these dials there are switches grouped in a slightly haphazard fashion. Cobra pedals are well placed and those for brake and throttle feature cast-in AC logos in their centre – the only ready reference you'll find to the company that built the cars for Shelby.

The early cars, including CSX2000, CSX2001 and CSX2002, featured Lucas electrics and Smiths gauges, while those from CSX2201 onwards were equipped with Ford electrics and Stewart Warner gauges. The area on the passenger side comprises a generous-sized lockable glovebox flanked by a chromed grab handle for the benefit of a white-knuckled passenger.

The interiors of CSX2000 and CSX2001 remain remarkably original whereas that of CSX2002, a competition car from birth, is inevitably more stripped-out and workmanlike. All three cars currently feature a single roll hoop on the driver's side with a brace bar terminating in the passenger footwell. The glovebox lid of CSX2001 is dominated by Carroll Shelby's autograph.

Technical analysis

Engine

The first product of Ford's innovative new thin-wall casting technique, introduced for 1962 as an option on the company's Fairlane and Mercury Meteor models, had a capacity of 221cu.in. (3.6 litre) and it was this unit the company initially agreed to supply Shelby for the Cobra. However, the larger 260cu.in. (4.2 litre) version was arriving on stream just as Shelby's project was coming to fruition, and it was a 260 that was installed in the prototype by Shelby American when it reached Santa Fe Springs, also in CSX2001 on its arrival in Pittsburgh and in CSX2002 before it first hit the race tracks.

Though not designed as a racing powerplant, the Windsor family of 90deg. V8 engines was nevertheless to prove pretty handy in the heat of competition. The thin-wall casting process meant the iron components were little heavier than all-alloy equivalents. In 260 form, it was over-square with a bore of 96.5mm (3.8in.) and stroke of 73mm (2.87in.) and, as fitted to the rally version of the Ford Falcon and Comet and the Cobra, benefited from Ford's HiPo specification of higher compression ratio, sportier camshaft, solid lifters rather than hydraulic tappets, superior cylinder head porting, and a four-barrel carburettor. The result was an output of 260bhp at 5,800rpm and 269lb.ft. torque at 4,800rpm – more than double that of the Bristol-engined Aces.

However, development never ceases in the automotive world and nor does the yen for more performance, and by September 1963 Shelby was starting to fit the latest version of Ford's Windsor engine in place of the original 260 unit. The stroke remained unchanged at 73mm (2.87in.), but the bore was increased to 101.6mm (4.00in.) to give a new capacity of 289cu.in. (4.7 litre). As chassis were not necessarily completed in numerical order, it is hard to chronicle the exact time of the change, but suffice to say the first 75 cars or so started life with the 260 engine, while the remaining leaf spring ones were powered by the 289. However, as it was in Ford's and Shelby's interest to have all Cobras giving optimum performance, and if any of the early cars succumbed to engine problems, the unit was often replaced with a 289 free-of-charge – as is understood to have been the case with CSX2001. Other cars were voluntarily upgraded by owners keen to keep abreast of the times and benefit from any power increase on offer. As a result, Cobras complete with their original 260 engine are now few and far between. The output of the standard 289 was 271bhp at 6,000rpm and 312lb.ft. at 3,400rpm.

It was around the time that the road cars began benefiting from the 289 engine that Shelby commenced the search for something considerably more powerful for the race track – a unit that would more than counter even the upcoming Ferrari LM and Grand Sport Corvette. Ford's NASCAR-proven 427cu.in. V8 was the powerplant of choice, but by dropping one into CSX2196 Ken Miles had conclusively proved that, while the venerable leaf spring chassis had coped manfully with up to a 171 per cent rise in horsepower, the jump to the 385 per cent available from a 427 engine in race tune was a step too far.

By the time the replacement coil spring chassis had been designed and put into production, a year had been lost, during which the Ford-powered Daytona Cobra Coupe, Mustang GT350 and GT40 had all become available for competition duty, and the 427 Cobra had been overtaken by events as far as international racing was concerned. It did, however, prove itself pretty unbeatable in national US events for a while, and in road terms was suddenly the datum by which the performance of all other cars was judged. *Car and Driver*'s test of a standard road version recorded a 0-60mph time of 4.3 seconds and a 0-100mph one of 8.8 seconds; though perhaps even more astonishing was

Considering a Cobra's engine bay is the same as the Ace that initially housed a 100bhp straight-six AC engine, Ford's thin-wall V8 is a remarkably perfect fit, and looks particularly splendid when topped by a quartet of IDA Webers, as in CSX2001.
Peter Harholdt

Technical analysis

the 0-100-0mph time achieved by Ken Miles on road tyres of a mere 13.2 seconds!

There were various permutations of the 427 engine, but what is not widely appreciated is that more than 100 of the 316 so-called 427 models produced were in fact powered by the related but less robust and less powerful Police Interceptor 428cu.in. unit. This situation reputedly resulted from supply problems of the 427 engine but it appears not all dealers rushed to inform customers if their car was of the lesser specification. This would have aided the Shelby coffers, as the 428 unit was much cheaper than its more sophisticated 427 sibling.

CSX2000 retains its original single-carburettor 260cu. in. engine, while CSX2001 and CSX2002 both have 289 engines fed by a quartet of Weber carburettors, as ultimately used by them in competition in the 1960s.

Transmission

From the outset, the standard transmission for the small-block Cobra was the ubiquitous Borg Warner T10 four-speed manual unit that at one time or another was

- The standard gearchange for the Borg Warner T10 unit fitted to 289 Cobras is this stubby but highly effective lever. Reverse is engaged by using the two prongs to lift a surrounding collar.
Peter Harholdt

- Close-up shows the rear suspension tower of a Cobra 289, the mounting of the leaf spring, the location of the wishbones, and how the Salisbury differential is firmly mounted to the chassis.
North Devon Metalcraft

employed by Ford, General Motors, AMC and Chrysler from 1957 into the 1980s. The T10s fitted to the 260 and early street 289 Cobras were equipped with cast-iron cases and tail-shafts, while competition cars and later 289 production models ran aluminium ones.

The standard gearchange lever was a stubby affair with an outer sleeve that was raised to allow reverse gear selection. A taller, sturdier-feeling Hurst shifter was available as a factory option. The gear sets of the alloy-cased boxes were interchangeable. Broadly speaking, road cars were equipped with either the L set (first, 2.36:1; second 1.76:1; third, 1.41:1; fourth 1:1) or later M set (first, 2.36:1; second, 1.62:1; third, 1.20:1; fourth, 1:1), while some racers opted for the K set that featured General Motors internals and related clutch plate. CSX2000, CSX2001 and CSX2002 would all have started life with cast-iron-cased T10 gearboxes.

Big-block (427) Cobras drove through Ford's own Top Loader four-speed manual unit – so-called because, instead of being located on the side as with the T10 and most other gearboxes of the time, the access plate for the internal workings was mounted on the top of the casing. The design was regarded as more rigid and therefore robust than the T10, and has therefore been retro-fitted by some latter-day 289 owners; especially those involved in competition.

Due to the extra length of the big-block engine, their gearboxes sat further back in the chassis, so their gearchange levers were cunningly reversed, thereby ensuring the gear knob was still in the right position for the driver. Though it might seem anathema to most enthusiast drivers, automatic transmission was an option for the 289 Cobra and some 20-30 examples were equipped from new with Ford's C-4 three-speed self-changing unit. However, most have subsequently been replaced with manual gearboxes and an original automatic gearbox Cobra is now a rare beast. Linking the manual gearboxes to the rear axle was one of the shortest prop-shafts on record – circa 10in. depending on the engine/transmission specification.

It is fair to say the ENV differential of the venerable AC Ace would never have coped with the torque of a 289 Cobra let alone a 427, so the model was equipped from the outset with essentially the same Salisbury 4HU final drive unit as Jaguar's MkX and E-type models – the only fundamental difference in the castings were the four bolt holes via which the nose of the unit was secured to the cross-member of the Cobra's chassis. The final drive ratio of the limited slip differential was 3.54:1 on the early cars that was later lowered to 3.77:1 – this had the effect of reducing the top speed a tad but improving acceleration times. Finally, as one might expect, a heftier pair of drive-shafts was employed to cope with the torque of the 427 engine. The transmission specifications of CSX2000, CSX2001 and CSX2002 have remained basically unchanged from the 1960s.

Suspension

As explained earlier, the Cobra's initial suspension system was a mildly modified version of that on which the AC Ace relied. It comprised transverse leaf springs front and rear allied to lower wishbones and telescopic dampers and actually worked surprisingly well up to a certain level, but the inherent changes of camber were a problem in out-and-out competition. As a result, the race

Head-on shot of a 289 chassis gives us a superior view of the front suspension and how the leaf spring affixes to the suspension tower and links to the lower wishbones via cast uprights – worm and sector steered cars featured fabricated front uprights.
North Devon Metalcraft

cars quickly received stiffer springs and dampers, anti-roll bars, and ever-wider wheels and tyres.

It is amazing what development can achieve in the hands of such talent as Ken Miles and Phil Remington, and in the last race of the 1963 season, Dan Gurney and Ken Miles finished a mighty impressive 1-2 at Long Island's Bridgehampton circuit, achieving the first FIA victory for an American car and driver and the first for a Ford-powered car at an FIA-sanctioned meeting.

Technical analysis

Here we see an example of the coil spring chassis that was primarily developed for the 427 engine. It is a clever uprate of the original Tojeiro design, that in AC 289 guise is thought by many to achieve the best ride/handling compromise of all Cobras.
Private collection

Following Ken Miles's heart-stopping experiences with the 427 pre-production prototype, it was decided a major revision of the chassis was required if a 427 Cobra was to become reality. A clever revamp was created, rather than a completely new design. At the time, Shelby's promotional material made much play of how Ford's suspension guru Klaus Arning and the Blue Oval's super-duper new computer had provided the answer. The facts are somewhat different, and the final format owed as least as much to the knowledge and patience of AC's Chief Engineer Alan Turner. Ultimately, the general layout of the twin-tube ladder chassis was retained, but the original 3in. chassis tubes were replaced by 4in. ones, set two and a half inches further apart. Gone were the 'cart' springs that Shelby had so abhorred and in their place were double wishbones and coil springs at each corner, plus trailing arms to help keep the back wheels pointing in the right direction. Anti-roll bars, though still not standard equipment, were fitted to the S/C and competition cars.

Steering

The only tangible difference between the Ace 2.6 steering and that of the early Cobras was the slight re-routing of the column to bypass the latter's wider V8 engine. In every other way the worm-and-sector system remained unchanged. Had AC been given more time to bring the Cobra to fruition, it is likely it would have featured a rack-and-pinion set-up from the outset – something the company had already used in the Greyhound four-seater. From a racing point of view there was no comparison between the two steering systems, as Ken Miles proved by using a rack-and-pinion-equipped car to knock two seconds off his Cobra record around the Riverside Raceway. It proved to be much more positive in the middle of a turn, while the simpler linkage resulted in less bump- and roll-steer, and therefore superior adhesion and general control.

The inevitable upgrade therefore came in April 1963, with the first car so equipped being CSX2126, and with the new system came a revised front suspension tower and superior front suspension set-up, complete with new cast, as opposed to fabricated, uprights. Although the change resulted in slightly heavier steering at parking speeds, many Cobra owners regarded the move as significant as that from the 260 to 289 engine. In the same way that a number of 260–engined cars these days sport 289 power, quite a few worm-and-sector ones now have rack-and-pinion steering; a modification CSX2001 is considered to have uniquely benefited from in period. To distinguish a worm-and-sector car from a rack-and-pinion one generally requires no more than a glance at the steering wheel – the former have flat rims with equally-spaced spokes, while the latter have dished rims with asymmetrically-spaced spokes, and they are not interchangeable.

Braking

As previously mentioned, much to AC's surprise, Shelby specified inboard rear disc brakes for his prototype Cobra. The major advantage of such a set-up is of course a notable reduction in unsprung weight, but it is never a win-win situation, and the potential disadvantages include poorer cooling and inferior access for servicing, making the rapid pad changes required in long distance racing a much harder job. In the end he settled for outboard Girling units all round on the production cars – 11.68in. (296mm) front and 10.75in. (273mm) at the rear. Perhaps surprisingly, the size of the production discs was never increased, even for keeping the far greater performance of the 427 models in check. What did change was that the original two-pot iron calipers on the front gave way to three-pot ones from CSX2125 onwards, and alloy calipers featured all round on the later racing cars and 427 S/C models. So, while some race cars certainly sported bigger brakes, it would appear that no production Cobra ever left the factory with 12in. brake discs front or rear, even though the Shelby brochure claimed that they were standard equipment from day one!

Wheels/tyres

All 260 and 289-engined Cobras started life on steel wire wheels – 5.5 x 15in. prior to CSX2160 and 6 x 15 in. thereafter. This in turn resulted in an increase in the flaring of the wheel arches and coincided with the introduction of the engine vents in the front wings. 427 models, on the other hand, were either equipped with Halibrand magnesium wheels or the 10-spoke so-called Sunburst alloys designed by Peter Brock. Halibrands were also de rigueur on all but the very early works race cars. As far as tyres are concerned, the Stateside cars were generally shod with Goodyear rubber, as a result of Shelby holding the Californian agency for that make, while Cobras and AC 289s destined for the UK or mainland European markets were usually equipped with Dunlop SP tyres.

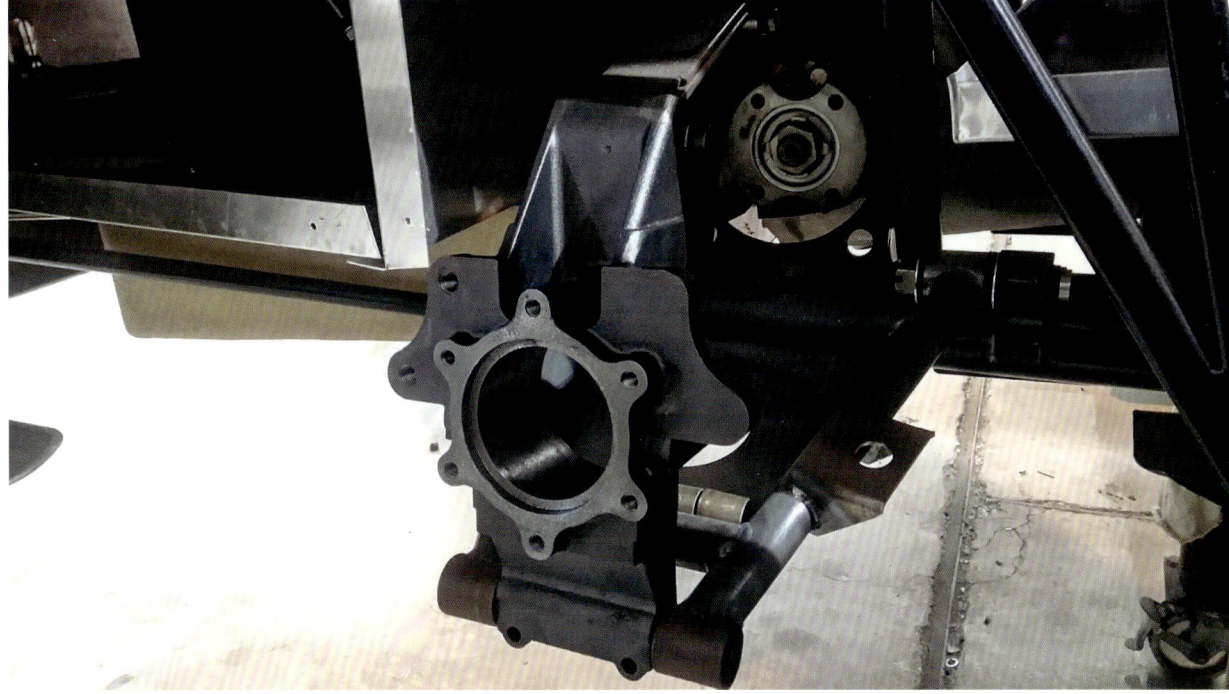

Top: The front corner of a 289 Cobra clearly displaying the wishbone and splined hub complete with steering arm. The wheels are retained by knock-off spinners. Right: A rear corner of a 289 Cobra showing how the top of the cast upright connects to the leaf spring and its lower end to the wishbone below.
North Devon Metalcraft

Part 2
CSX2000

● The one and only prototype Cobra as it stands today, in remarkably original, unmolested condition. It caused a sensation at its introduction in spring 1962 and again when it sold for $13.75 million in 2016.
Robin Adams

No doubt to some soulless individuals, CSX2000 is just another motor car. But those imbued with the backstory of Shelby's dream will appreciate that the one and only prototype Cobra is the metallic embodiment of the aspirations of a great many impassioned individuals.

For Shelby and his disciples it was tangible proof that Carroll's determination to echo the path of Allard and Healey by shoe-horning American V8 muscle into the nose of a British-designed and built chassis really could make production sense, while for AC it represented the possibility of injecting new life into a model that was otherwise past its prime. For Ford, it promised to provide the solution to the company's ever-more thorny problem of countering Chevrolet both in the showroom and on the track. And let's not forget the ever-growing band of car-mad enthusiasts who were desperate to nail their flag to whichever brand could make their heart beat fastest. Yes, if CSX2000 was a human being, it would probably have quickly crumbled under the phenomenal weight of expectation that surrounded it from birth.

But it's not (quite) human, and not only single-handedly kick-started the Cobra phenomenon, but remained in its maker's personal care until his death. We review the first 55 years of the remarkably original Cobra prototype.

Chapter 4
The one and only prototype

It is usual for production versions of a car as successful as the Cobra to be preceded by just one prototype, but it is important to remember that, far from being a new design, Shelby's dream was based on an existing, well-proven sports car – the AC Ace. Moreover, and contrary to much that was written in period, the version concerned was not the Bristol-engined Ace, but the 2.6-litre Ford Zephyr-powered variant that already featured some of the modifications now commonly, but erroneously, attributed to the Cobra project. These include: the lowering and lengthening of the front bodywork and the consequent narrowing of the radiator grille, plus the installation of more substantial kingpins.

For the record, the salient differences between the chassis and body of a 2.6-litre Ace and the prototype Cobra are:

- Thicker-walled tubing for the main chassis rails (13 SWG instead of 14 SWG) and an additional cross member ahead of the rear axle to support the nose of the new, meatier Salisbury differential unit.
- Longer/stiffer suspension leaves; longer/stronger wishbones and a consequent 2in.increase in track front and rear.
- A redesign of the rear suspension tower in order to carry the Salisbury 4HU differential in place of the old ENV unit.
- Sand-cast ductile iron rear suspension uprights in place of fabricated ones.
- Triple-laced 72-spoke 15in. wire wheels in place of the Ace's 16in. rims.
- Repositioned steering box to allow the column to clear the extra width of the V8 engine.
- The addition of subtle wheelarch 'eyebrows' to take account of the wider track.

The major features that distinguish CSX2000 from all subsequent Cobras include:

- Brakes – it was the only example built with inboard rear brakes. Production cars had outboard discs all round – generally, 11.68in. front and 10.75in.rear.
- Its fuel tank was positioned below the boot whereas on production cars it was mounted above the rear axle, improving stability and allowing the spare wheel to be housed in the boot floor, which in turn increased luggage space.
- Fuel filler – this is located on the nearside rear flank. Production 260/289 road cars had them centrally-mounted behind the seats, while on 427 models they were located on the offside rear flank.
- It had Ace over-riders and boot lid – the production cars featured slightly more substantial over-riders (and often full width 'nudge' bars as well) and a shorter lid.

As stated earlier, AC completed CSX2000 in just three months, an astonishing tribute to the team in Thames Ditton. Reports of testing vary from Carroll Shelby driving the car at Silverstone and/or the MIRA proving ground, to no more than a quick squirt by AC staff around the roads near the factory. Whatever the truth, there can have been precious little time for such activity before Shelby's baby was stripped of its

A fine view of CSX2000, this time with the man himself at the wheel. It was reputedly one of the few automotive treasures Carroll Shelby retained to his death. It is not hard to see why the attachment was so enduring.
Private collection

46 | Exceptional Cars

The one and only prototype

● CSX2000 was the only Cobra to feature inboard rear brakes, which can clearly be seen in this photo. Also visible is the Salisbury 4HU differential and notably short propshaft linking it to the car's Borg Warner T10 gearbox.
Private collection

● According to renowned photographer Dave Friedman, who recorded CSX2000's assembly for posterity, the feat was achieved in just eight hours. Here the engine is in and the job looks well on the way to completion.
The Henry Ford/Dave Friedman

trial engine and transmission and air-freighted to Los Angeles on 20 February. From LA airport it was trailered to Shelby American's makeshift home in Santa Fe Springs, where it was immediately jumped upon by Dean Moon's eager band of Californian hot-rodders.

Shelby was so confident in his new 'sport' car that he was determined to show it to the media in the fastest possible time. Crack photographer Dave Friedman recorded the car's assembly for posterity and timed it at a mere eight hours, at which point Shelby and Moon immediately took to the nearby roads, about which Moon reputedly said: 'We got drunk and drove it around an impromptu course we'd set up between the oil derricks. When it didn't break even after all that rough treatment, well, then we knew we had a good car.'

The trial engine used by AC Cars was almost certainly a 221cu.in. unit (AC certainly thought so and, as the Cobra name had yet to be coined, referred to it as the Ace 3.6 – the litre equivalent of 221cu.in.), whereas the one installed in Santa Fe Springs was a 260cu.in. HiPo version as fitted to Falcon Sprints, that featured solid lifters rather than hydraulic tappets, gas-flowed heads and breathed through a four-barrel Holley carburettor. The output was 260bhp – rather neatly, 1 horsepower per cubic inch.

A notable point about CSX2000 at this stage is that it was presented in unpainted aluminium, and the team reputedly used up a whole box of Brillo pads and hours of elbow grease in order to ready the car for the press. With no official company decals yet available, 'Shelby' was hastily sign-written in large letters on the nose and tail, and 'Powered by Ford' slogans applied to the front wings.

48 | Exceptional Cars

The one and only prototype

One of Shelby's many hats of the time was that of contributor to *Sports Car Graphic* magazine, so it is no surprise that the magazine's editor, John Christy, was the first journalist to sample the beast first-hand. His unequivocal conclusion was: 'it is one of the most impressive production sports cars we've ever driven.' For the next few months, the wire wheels of CSX2000 barely stopped turning. Being the only example in the world, it was press car, development hack, show pony and sales demonstrator all rolled into one. And thank goodness nobody crashed it, as could so easily have been the case, as it is questionable if the project could have recovered from the consequences; so hand-to-mouth were those early days.

CSX2000's first major public viewing was the New York Auto Show in April, for which it was sprayed in a vivid shade of pearlescent yellow – Dean Moon reputedly advised it was a perfect hue for display under strip lights. Right or wrong, the car was a major hit with the Ford dealers and public alike and *Road & Track*'s coverage stated 'just this side of reality falls the Shelby Cobra which, if not stillborn, could take the sports car world by storm.' The Shelby bandwagon was starting to roll and, when the same publication first tested the car, they boosted its profile further by recording the astounding figures of 0-60mph in 4.2 seconds, 0-100 in 10.8 seconds, a standing quarter mile time of 13.8 seconds, and a top speed of no less than 153mph. These were impressive results even by today's standards and, it has to be said, not readily repeated by subsequent road tests, leading some to question whether the engine was perhaps of a slightly higher specification than declared – an echo of the stunt Jaguar famously pulled with the E-type.

Talking of stunts, one of many oft-repeated stories to emanate from the Shelby camp over the years was that, in order to disguise the fact that for five months there was only one Cobra in the entire world, CSX2000 was resprayed a different colour every time it was presented for a press test, thereby giving the impression that far more cars had been produced and the programme was way more advanced than was actually the case. It is a fabulous tale, but one also open to dispute. The car as it stands today – resplendent in its final livery of metallic blue, is completely unrestored and not without the odd war wound, one of which has revealed a large square of a different hue below the blue. It is not red, green or any of the other shades supposedly used at one time or another, but yellow, as seen in New York way back in April 1962!

Once the production vehicles started to come on stream, CSX2000's role shrank from 'star of the show' to that of 'occasional extra', and for a while it served as one of the instruction cars at Shelby's driving school at the Riverside Raceway, before reputedly being placed

Sports Car Graphic was the first magazine to get behind the wheel of CSX2000. Note the hastily contrived lettering on the nose, AC Ace over-riders, and the 5.5 inch wheels that were fitted to this and the first production Cobras.
Private collection

The one and only prototype

- CSX2000 serving as a course car at the Riverside Raceway, California in March 1962 – the track at which the first works race car, CSX2002, would make its memorable debut seven months later.
Private collection

- By putting a fifth wheel on the prototype, *Sports Car Graphic* magazine quickly confirmed their suspicions that it was the fastest accelerating production sports car they had ever tested. Their 0-60mph figure was 4.2 seconds.
Private collection

in long-term storage. Nobody in authority seems to recall exactly when it received its current livery, so we can assume it was a while ago. One would also imagine it has covered relatively few miles from new, as for the last 50 years it has done little other than represent the brand at exhibitions, race meetings and key anniversaries – not least the Cobra 50th birthday celebrations of 2012 at Pebble Beach, California, and the New York Auto Show.

The car's primary residence for the last two decades of semi-retirement was the Shelby headquarters in Las Vegas, and Carroll's grandson Aaron is among those who's amazed his grandfather kept it all that time – 'not from a money perspective, but because he got rid of so many things over the years.' Well, for whatever reason, CSX2000 was not one of them, and in 1983

Carroll established the Carroll Shelby Trust, into which he placed his various trademarks and properties, plus the prototype Cobra. The intention of the Trust was to support the Carroll Shelby Foundation, which benefits the Children's Organ Transplant Association, the Eli Home for abused children, the Carroll Shelby School of Automotive Technology, and the Carroll Shelby Automotive Museum in Gardena, California.

Some years before he died, Shelby agreed that, when the trustees felt the time was right, his friend Rob Myers of RM Auctions should put the car up for sale, but not before. With the exponential rise in classic car values, it was decided to press the button in 2016, and one of the world's most famous and desirable sports cars came to market at RM's annual Monterey sale on 19 August. Fittingly, it was driven onto the stage by Aaron

The one and only prototype

Shelby, and when the hammer finally fell, the Trust was better off to the tune of $13.75 million. The successful bidder was Greg Miller, who had purchased it to add to the already astonishing collection of Shelby-related vehicles established by his late father Larry Miller. Its illustrious stablemates include: Cobra CSX2002 – covered in depth elsewhere in this book; CSX2019 – the first Dragonsnake Cobra; CSX2299 – the second of only six Daytona Cobra Coupes; P1015 – the GT40 MkII that finished second at Le Mans in 1966 in the hands of Ken Miles and Denny Hulme; and J-4 – the MkIV GT40 that won the 12 Hours of Sebring in 1967. The cars are not currently displayed *en masse*, but a new museum is planned for the future. In the meantime CSX2000 can sometimes be seen at the Shelby American Museum in Boulder, Colorado.

- Another striking view of CSX2000. Points of note are the early-style rectangular rear badge, AC Ace over-riders and the long Ace boot lid – a shorter version of which was fitted to production Cobras from day one.
Private collection

- The September 1962 issue of *Road & Track* carried a full road test of CSX2000, which also dominated the front cover. By then its once polished aluminium body had been painted a strident shade of pearlescent yellow.
Private collection

The First Three Shelby Cobras | 51

The one and only prototype

● A landmark day for Planet Cobra occurred on 19 August 2016 when CSX2000 sold at auction for $13.75 million. It now forms part of the Larry Miller Collection alongside many other famous Shelby-inspired cars.
RM Auctions/Sotheby's

was born - while under the bonnet lie the car's original pair of 'home' fabricated exhaust manifolds and even a Delaney-Gallay radiator of the type so quickly superseded in production.

The speedometer is believed to be the one hastily sourced when the car was first assembled and reputedly started life in a Mercedes! The leather-trimmed driver's seat looks as though it's been home to a thousand mice, but only because it's been brushed by the trousers of countless aficionados, not least those of Mr Shelby himself – if this car could talk, it could doubtless spin some wonderful yarns. For sure, if invited, the restore/not restore fraternities would have a field day arguing over the fate of this automotive idol, but Greg Miller laid out his stall early on, to the relief of many an enthusiast: 'The worst possible thing we could do is restore it. It's got beautiful patina and, as discussed with Aaron Shelby, we intend to clean the car up and give it a thorough detailing. Our plans are for preservation only.' Amen!

CSX2000 in summary

There are so many facets to CSX2000 that justified its 2016 sale price of $13.75 million – or, some would say more still. The most obvious is that it is the daddy of the brand, the one and only prototype around which the Cobra legend was built.

Then there is its originality – it could so easily have been hacked around in the course of development or left in a corner to rot once its prime function had been superseded.

There is also the direct connection to the man himself, the one car that Carroll Shelby hung on to until his death despite disposing of so many other landmark items along the way. It is impossible to over-state the historical importance of this car to the automotive fraternity.

It is also worth reflecting that if the world had been denied CSX2000, there would have been no World Championship-winning Daytona Cobra Coupes; no 427 Cobra (the fastest accelerating sports car of its generation); no Shelby Mustangs and, who knows, the GT40 may never have won Le Mans. Few, if any other cars can claim such a golden legacy.

As is so often the case with cars of all types, the Cobra grew with age and a competition 427 is a very different looking beast to CSX2000, which possesses such a purity of line and displays little evidence of the might that lies within. It still rides on painted 5.5in. wire wheels and is free of such impedimenta as nudge bars, wing mirrors and any other non-essential accessories, with the very sensible exception of a roll hoop. The badging is limited to one of the original rectangular Shelby AC Cobra ones front and rear and 'Powered By Ford' signs on the front flanks. Hidden below the surface is that unique pair of inboard rear brakes – the Shelby whim that was overturned before even CSX2001

Photo gallery

Studio photography by Robin Adams

The one and only prototype

● From this angle, only the oblong Shelby badge and the discreet flaring of the wheelarches distinguish CSX2000 from the AC Ace 2.6 that sired it. It is a different story when the engine chimes into life!

● Above left: XJJ 292 – the California registration familiar to all Cobra aficionados. Above: Note how the carpet has been worn down by many a heavy throttle foot. Left: The flat wood-rim steering wheel has equally spaced spokes.

Above: The rev-counter is arguably the most important instrument for any sports car. Above right: The Cobra's well-stocked dashboard. Right: The leather of the unrestored seat has been brushed by the trousers of numerous famous drivers.

- Above left: The lightly flared wheelarch and painted 15-inch wire wheel are clearly visible. Above: The period rear-view mirror atop the facia. Left: The alloy expansion tank under the bonnet – cooling was an issue in the Cobra's early days.

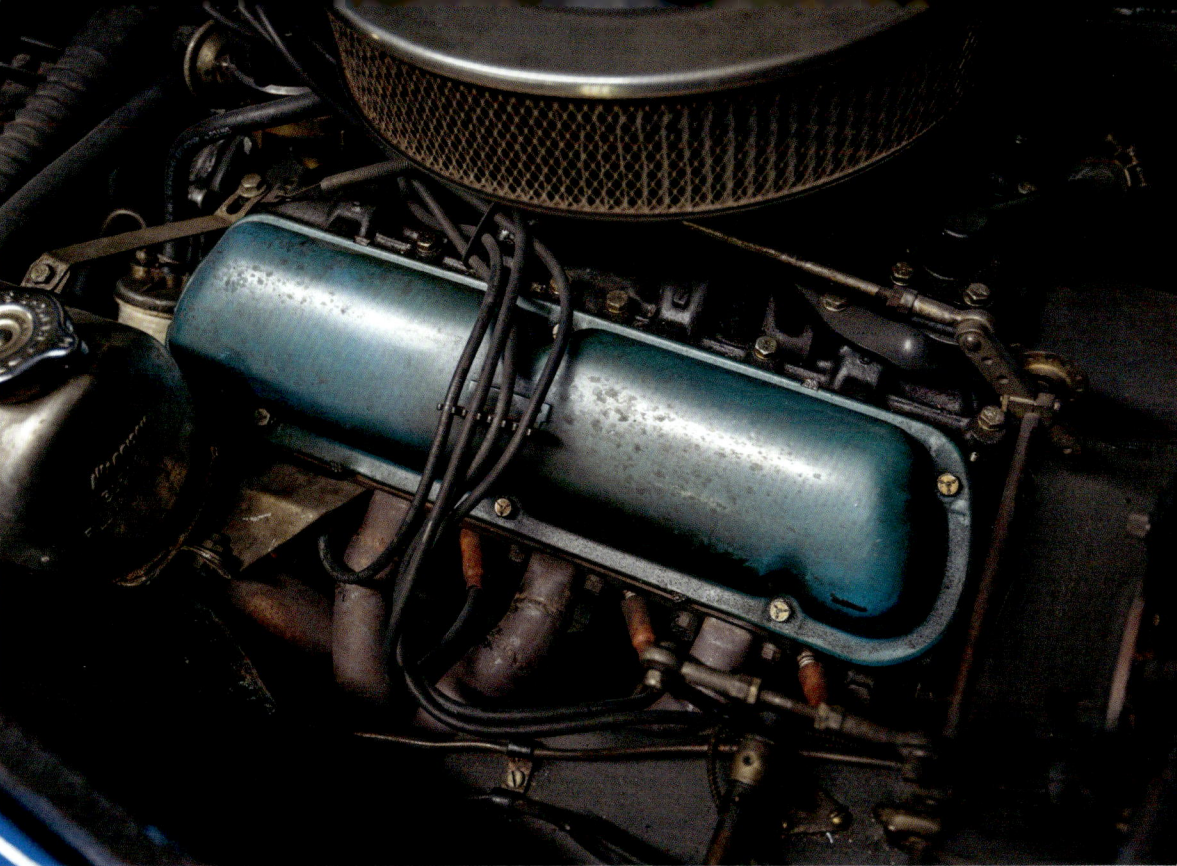

Above: The throttle linkage and fundamental electrics. Above right: the 260 HiPo engine complete with its original, hastily fabricated exhaust manifolds. Right: The fully trimmed boot area – one of the few touches not carried through to production.

● From whichever angle you study it, the prototype Cobra strikes a graceful but purposeful pose. Some prefer the purity of its lines to those of the later, wider cars, while other enthusiasts view a racing 427 as the ultimate incarnation of the breed.

The First Three Shelby Cobras

Part 3
CSX2001

One could argue that CSX2001, the first production example, is at least as important as the prototype, as it quietly racked up a succession of milestones for Shelby's embryo company. For example: it was the first Cobra to be assembled and sold by Ed Hugus's European Cars, Pittsburgh, Pennsylvania, the first ever entered for a race (be it without the knowledge or permission of Shelby American!), one of only four Shelby roadsters to circulate Le Circuit de la Sarthe in period, and the only one ever to contest the still more demanding Tour de France. It was also probably the first 260-engined example to have its powerplant exchanged for a 289 unit, and the first privately owned Cobra to be retro-fitted with rack-and-pinion steering.

Its colourful European history includes administrative assistance from Stirling Moss, a magazine colour shoot with French heart-throb Johnny Hallyday, and a decade masquerading as the Cobra it had sometimes competed against in 1964 – COX6010. Its years in the hands of Jean Marie Vincent were punctuated by a unique hardtop, bonnet and front sidelights, plus the rear flaring of the doors that this remarkably original Cobra retains to this day.

🟡 CSX2001 was the first production Cobra but, like so many examples of the breed, was soon put to work on the track, and carved out an enviable reputation on the race circuits and hill-climbs of France. It is now part of Bruce Meyer's renowned private collection.
Peter Harholdt

Chapter 5
The first production Cobra

There were just five months between the fanfare of the prototype arriving at Dean Moon's garage in Santa Fe Springs, California and CSX2001 taking to the roads of Pittsburgh, no less than 2,422 miles away. Finished in red, it came off the line at AC Cars, Thames Ditton in the UK, on 17 July 1962, and was then air-freighted from London to New York before being trailered the 370 miles to European Cars. Like CSX2000, it arrived complete with AC badges front and rear but, whereas Shelby didn't want any reference to AC on the exterior of the Cobras (though seemingly had no problem with the logo being cast into the pedals), Hugus was keen to emphasise the newcomer's parentage, and therefore not only retained the Thames Ditton-supplied AC emblems but added the strange temporary Cobra badges supplied by Shelby.

The main task was to install its 260 engine and Borg Warner T10 transmission and turn the vehicle into a running concern. The second one was to find a buyer for the car but also, with an eye on the bigger picture, use it to help market the Cobra brand and thereby ensure continuing sales down the line. With that, Hugus foresaw a problem. At first glance, an early Shelby Cobra looked remarkably similar to the AC Ace from which it was sired and to the untrained eye revealed little of its far superior performance potential. He saw part of the answer as getting on track and proving its worth before a knowledgeable crowd.

The selected meeting was on 26 August at nearby Connellsville Airport, by which time CSX2001 had been equipped with a roll bar. The bar's distinctive design was unique to a handful of Cobras assembled by European Cars. Unlike most such devices, it spanned the entire centre section of the car. This instantly recognisable accessory was to remain a feature of CSX2001 for many years to come.

As Hugus was about to discover, the Ace-style Delaney-Gallay radiators fitted to the first few Cobras had insufficient flow to cool a 4.2-litre V8 engine in the heat of competition, and he retired from the meeting after only a few laps. It was a somewhat ignominious episode which would have done little to improve his relationship with Shelby, which was reputedly already on the wane. Temporarily banned from further competition, the car's next public showing was at the Pittsburgh Auto Show on 15 October.

By now a buyer had been found in the form of psychiatrist Richard Milo. A long-standing acquaintance of Ed Hugus, the good doctor was a keen amateur racer of the perfect background – his CV included a class win at Sebring in an AC Ace – and he took delivery of the car before the turn of the year. His son David Milo was no more than 10 at the time, but vividly remembers seeing the speedo register 120mph on a nearby unopened freeway and his mother performing power turns with the car. There were inevitably teething problems, and David's stepbrother, another Richard Milo, particularly recalls the tendency of the engine to overheat, for which attempted cures included the installation of a trio of Volkswagen Beetle chrome grilles to the rear of the bonnet. Shelby American's solution included the replacement of the original 260 unit with one of the very early 289s (a notion supported by the advert used to sell the car at a later date).

CSX2001 in its racing heyday. Here Frenchman Jean Marie Vincent prepares to tackle the Normandy hill-climb Course de Côte des Andelys. He enjoyed much success in such events during 1964 and 1965, but had to settle for second in class on this occasion.
Private collection

The first production Cobra

It seems that, although entries were made for SCCA regional races at Dunkirk (New York) and Watkins Glen (New York), Milo Senior's only documented competition outing in the car was at Connellsville on 10/11 August 1963. Clearly the beast and this track did not see eye-to-eye, for it failed to finish on this visit too; this time as a result of a high-speed blow-out of one of its Goodyear Blue Streak tyres. According to David Milo: 'This incident frightened my dad sufficiently for him to totally reconsider the idea of racing, and the tyre, complete with large egg-shaped hole, remained in the garage as a reminder for years to come.' Richard Milo never used the Cobra in anger again and it was sold to Lloyd 'Lucky' Casner from the well-known Camoradi racing team. Whether Casner ever intended to take delivery of the car is unclear, but as things turned out its title swiftly passed to French airline pilot Jean Marie Vincent. Richard Milo Junior well remembers accompanying his father on the journey from Pittsburgh to New York in the Cobra prior to its freighting to France.

Jean Marie Vincent had no experience of the Cobra or Le Mans when he was initially forced to tackle the track in torrential rain during the 1964 April Le Mans Trial. In drier conditions he achieved the 20th fastest time of the weekend.
Private collection

Later on the Sunday of the Le Mans Trial and conditions have clearly improved. All things considered, Vincent's times were good. Nevertheless he chose to have the car uprated for subsequent events rather than contest the Le Mans 24 Hours two months later.
Private collection

The first production Cobra

Paris-based Vincent had registered some reasonable results at his local circuit, Montlhéry, in the early 1960s at the wheel of such medium-powered racers as a Bristol-engined AC Ace and Fiat Abarth 700, but had designs on international competition and, like his friend the Baron Jean de Mortemart, had witnessed the Hugus-run Cobra CSX2142 and class-winning CS2131 compete at Le Mans in 1963, and become desperate to have one of his own. The problem was, none were immediately available outside the US at the time and his enquiries led him via AC Cars to Hugus and then Casner.

The original plan was for Vincent to share his new acquisition with Casner in the 1964 Le Mans 24 Hour race. But, come the time of the official Trial, 18/19 April, there was no sign of his co-driver or the Cobra. Vincent recalled: 'In the week running up to the event I scoured the cargo holds of every plane flying from the US. Alas, not even a hint of a Cobra wheel spinner, and it wasn't until 3.00am on the last morning of the Trial that it had finally been unearthed from the hold of a TWA Boeing and placed on French soil. Hallelujah!

'I connected the plug leads (thanks to a customs officer who knew the firing order of a V8 Ford, which I will now never forget) and fired up the engine – ah,

- Following the Le Mans Trial, Vincent opted to tackle the Coupes de l'USA meeting at Montlhéry, but was forced into retirement by boiling brake fluid. Note the distinctive roll bar – as fitted by European Cars in Pittsburgh. *Private collection*

- High-ranking company – CSX2001 in *parc fermé* on the 1964 Tour de France Automobile, sandwiched between the Trintignant/Saint-Auban Cobra Coupe and the Ferrari 250 GTO of Piper and Siffert. *Private collection*

66 | Exceptional Cars

the sound of a V8 at night in the middle of the airport! By 4.30am I was on my way to Le Mans on lovely dry weather tyres in the pouring rain. The torque of the beast was stunning and it seemed every time I touched the throttle my snake took off – there were an incalculable number of spins.'

After two sleepless nights and the journey of a lifetime, Vincent arrived at the circuit to discover Casner was not coming and he had to practice the car alone. Initially, it was pouring with rain so, having never experienced the track before, he erected the Shelby's rudimentary hood and followed Mortemart's Cobra (COX6010) for a few laps before venturing off on his own – 'the circuit was drenched, the car slid, and I felt about as comfortable as a cat in an Olympic swimming pool.' However his confidence grew, the rain ceased and, against all odds, he recorded the 20th fastest lap time, two places ahead of Mortemart and seven in front of Peter Bolton in the ill-fated Cobra-based AC A98 Coupe.

Exactly a week later, Vincent was back in the more familiar territory of Montlhéry for the Coupes de l'USA meeting. He was still finding the Cobra a handful, though, and reported experiencing no less than three spins in seven laps. Then the brake fluid was boiling and he had no option but to withdraw the car. Class victory went to the rival Cobra of his buddy Jean de Mortemart.

However, Vincent had always planned to treat his new racer to a major makeover and now was the obvious time. He masterminded the work which was largely carried out by the official French AC concessionaire, Garage de Lorraine, run by André Chardonnet. The aim was more power, more grip – more everything. The 289 engine was fully race prepared, during which the four-barrel Holley was replaced by a quartet of IDA Webers. The wire wheels were supplanted by a set of magnesium Halibrands (6.5in. front and 8.5in. rear) which required a substantial widening of the front and rear wheel arches. Uniquely, and unlike the Shelby FIA cars whose wider rear flares were accommodated by shortening the doors, those on the Vincent car were designed to commence in the doors themselves by curving their rear edges outwards. The original bonnet scoop was replaced by a large horizontal slot at its leading edge and a power bulge was created above the Webers. The 1963 Le Mans Cobras had both sported long-tailed hard-tops and were therefore the most likely inspiration for the bespoke one now fitted to CSX2001. Its design was slightly akin to the roof of the ensuing 1964 Ferrari 250 GTO, but even its proud owner had to admit it was visually challenging, though claimed it helped to increase the Cobra's top speed to 270km/h (168mph). Another modification unique to CSX2001 was the repositioning of the front sidelights that were moved outwards to accommodate a pair of powerful driving lights.

Along with the re-profiled doors, these features made the Vincent Cobra immediately recognisable during this salient period of its history. However, the most fundamental change of all lay hidden below. Cobras now leaving the factory featured rack-and-

CSX2001 garaged during the 1964 Tour de France, with the works Daytona Cobra Coupes of Simon/Dupeyron and Bondurant/Neerpasch. Of the 117 starters only 36 cars survived the notoriously tough event that year. Unfortunately, CSX2001 was not one of them.
Private collection

The first production Cobra

pinion steering rather than the original worm-and-sector setup still installed in CSX2001. At this stage, there was no precedent for retro-fitting the new system, but (reportedly with the help of Stirling Moss, AC's competition manager of the time) Vincent was provided with a new section of chassis from the engine mounts forwards, complete with the revised steering and related front suspension and dished steering wheel. This ensemble was collected from the Thames Ditton factory by Jean Marie himself and professionally grafted on to his car by the Garage de Lorraine shop foreman, Monsieur Columba, who was factory-trained to work on Cobras. Other upgrades are understood to have included bigger brakes, the installation of anti-roll bars front and rear, Koni dampers and a 36-gallon alloy fuel tank, as required for long distance events. By the time these major amendments were complete, the 1964 Le Mans race had been and gone and Vincent's focus had moved onto the annual Tour de France Automobile that took place in September.

To many minds, the Tour de France of the period

● A rear view of CSX2001 on the Tour de France, still wearing the Hugus-originated combination of Shelby and AC badges and its original Pennsylvania licence plate.
Private collection

● Before the Tour de France was over, Vincent had put disappointment behind him, got his car repaired and returned to the familiar surroundings of Montlhéry for the Coupes de Paris meeting. It resulted in his first victory with CSX2001.
Private collection

● Tour de France 1964. When hopes were still high, CSX2001 thunders round the Reims circuit. Clear to see are: the sidelights that were realigned to accommodate auxiliary spotlights; wide Halibrand wheels; and the uniquely flared doors.
Archives Maurice Louche

The first production Cobra

Vincent's first hill-climb aboard CSX2001 was the inaugural Course de Côte de La Pommeraye. Nowadays it is dominated by purpose-built machinery but in 1964 the Cobra was all-conquering, giving Vincent another deserved victory.
Private collection

was the biggest motor sport challenge in Europe and, at 10 days and over 8,000km, a far bigger test of man and machine than the Mille Miglia, Monte Carlo Rally, or even Le Mans. The 1964 event was the penultimate round of that year's World Sports Car Championship and comprised no less than eight circuit races and nine hill-climbs. It had numerous high-profile entries, including works cars from Ferrari, Porsche, Lancia, Alpine, BMC, Standard-Triumph and BMW, while keeping Vincent's Cobra company in the over 3-litre class were three Shelby Daytona Cobra Coupes – a Shelby American entry for Bob Bondurant and Jochen Neerpasch, and Ford France supported cars for Maurice Trintignant/Bernard de Saint-Auban and André Simon/Maurice Dupeyron. There should also have been a Cobra roadster for Guy Ligier and Henry Morrogh, but it failed to appear.

Some period reports show Casner as Vincent's co-driver on this occasion, but it was in fact fellow Frenchman Gerard Faget. Sadly, despite the many months of preparation, their heavily reconfigured Cobra did not behave as hoped. Even though the engine was reputedly out of tune from the outset, the crew survived the Reims race and finished a very creditable eighth overall up the Bramont hill-climb, but not long afterwards the car's differential cried enough and, in Vincent's own words, 'it was the height of disgrace when the rear deck shamefully fell on the floor.' It was poor reward for so brave an effort, but the pairing was far from alone in failing to finish; only 36 of 117 starters managed to last the whole 10 days. The retirements included every single entry in the over 3-litre class, though the Daytona Cobra Coupes had dominated the early stages. Overall victory in the event fell to the Ecurie Francorchamps 250 GTO of Lucien Bianchi and Georges Berger. So ended the first top-level test for both Vincent and CSX2001.

Despite what must have been a bitter disappointment, by the last day of the Tour de France, Vincent had already had the Cobra repaired and was back at Montlhéry for the non-championship Coupe de Paris meeting. On this occasion his opposition included the now familiar Cobra of his buddy de Mortemart, four Lotus Elans, three Abarth Simcas, two Fiat Abarths, a brace of Jaguar Mk2s, one Ford Galaxie, and a lone Porsche 356. The front row of the grid comprised the two Cobras sandwiching the quickest of the Elans, with Vincent on pole, from where he scored his and CSX2001's first victory. He finished no less than 47 seconds ahead of the Abarth-Simca of Claude Ballot-Léna and well clear of the de Mortemart Cobra back in fifth place.

For his next challenge, Vincent opted for a round of the French Hill-climb Championship – in fact the first ever run on the Course de Côte de La Pommeraye. The town of La Pommeraye is situated in the picturesque valley of the River Loire, 70km west of Nantes. Its hill-climb is still in operation 53 years on and is these days dominated by such purpose-built machines as the French designed and constructed Norma M20FC, but in 1964 the inaugural victory fell to one Jean Marie Vincent driving CSX2001.

His penultimate challenge for the 1964 season was yet another Montlhéry meeting, the 1000km de Paris, which took place on 11 October. On this occasion he was driving with rather than against his friend and fellow Cobra *pilote*, Jean de Mortemart. The event served as the 20th and final round of the World Sports Car Championship and therefore featured some top names at the wheel of serious machinery, including no less than five Ferrari GTOs, three Ferrari LMs and five Porsche 904s. First past the flag was the A-list pairing of Graham Hill and Jo Bonnier in a Maranello Concessionaires-entered Ferrari 330 P. Fortune didn't favour CSX2001 on this occasion – Vincent experienced a scary aquaplaning moment during the wet qualifying session and the pair started the race down in 18th position. Problems with the starter motor at the driver change eventually put them out of the running.

Vincent's first year of competition with CSX2001 ended with the Rallye de l'AGACI. This mixed discipline two-day event consisted of races at Rouen and Montlhéry, plus hill-climbs at La Bouille, Gondreville and Sermaise. This time around Jean Marie elected to share the Cobra with fellow countryman Franck Ruata and, despite some notably wet weather (not always popular with Cobra drivers), they between them won all five stages to take a convincing overall victory. There can surely be no better way to finish a season.

To open his 1965 competition calendar, Vincent returned to the French Hill-climb Championship and the Course de Côte d'Hébécrevon. By coincidence, it was from the tiny village of Hébécrevon on 25 July 1944 that the American army launched 'Operation Cobra' – the offensive that led to the collapse of the German front in Normandy, and it was on 3 July 1965 when Jean Marie Vincent began his two-day attempt at a Cobra victory in exactly the same place. The weather was not initially on anybody's side, but improved as

CSX2001 in full cry round the Montlhéry banking during the 1964 1000km de Paris. As the final round of the World Sports Car Championship the event featured many top drivers. Vincent shared the drive with Jean de Mortemart.
Private collection

In this photo, Vincent, crouching, appears to be assisting a scrutineer prior to the start of the event. The race was not a success for the French duo. Fighting back from 18th place on the grid, they were eventually sidelined by a problem with the starter motor.
Private collection

The first production Cobra

● Vincent opened his 1965 competition season with another hill-climb – the Course de Côte d'Hébécrevon. The weather initially favoured nobody, but once the rain ceased, Vincent removed the centre section of the infamous hardtop and secured another victory.
Private collection

the event progressed, encouraging the attendance of several thousand spectators and allowing Vincent to run with the centre section of the Cobra's infamous hardtop removed, Targa-style. His main opposition came from Bernard Lagier's Abarth-Simca and a pair of Lotuses, but ultimately it was another victory for Vincent and CSX2001.

Next up was another Normandy hill-climb, the Course de Côte des Andelys. The track had been extended from the previous year to 1.36km and was felt to be easier overall, if more dangerous in the final section. CSX2001 now had a new look – gone was that controversial hardtop, while a pair of wide white stripes now adorned the centre of the red car. The power of the Cobra would always be welcome on a race circuit, but by nature hill-climb courses tend to be tighter and twistier, where handling and manoeuvrability can sometimes count for more. That was certainly the case in this event, where overall victory went to Henri Grandsire in a single-seat Alpine and Vincent had to settle for second place in the GT class behind Swiss driver Denis Borel's Abarth-Simca.

Come 3 October and it was time to return to the Course de La Pommeraye, the scene of Vincent's first hill-climb triumph a year earlier. This time there were far more competitors, including Formula 3 single-seaters, so although all eyes were on the previous winner, it was going to be tough for Vincent to repeat the feat, and so it proved. Overall victory this time went to Patrice Gransart in an F3 Lotus-Ford, but Vincent did manage to annexe the GT class, beating the nimble Abarth-Simca of René Barone by three seconds.

For what would prove to be his last competitive outing with CSX2001, Vincent selected the Rallye de l'AGACI, another event he had won the year before. Ruata had proved to be a notably quick partner, so the pairing remained unchanged, but the competition was stronger than before and the racing was tough on cars and drivers alike. The Reims circuit saw the demise of both René-Louis Revillon's Ferrari GTO and the Vincent Cobra; its engine was off song and melted its sparking plugs. This left Jean-Michel Giorgi (Ferrari GTO – accompanied by eminent racing car photographer/sculptor Emmanuel Zurini) and the pairing of Jo Schlesser and Johnny Rives (Porsche 904 Carrera GTS) to fight for outright honours. Victory ultimately went to French national hero Schlesser, despite losing his clutch at the start of the final race at Montlhéry.

Vincent had blazed a unique trail with CSX2001, had a lot of enjoyment and no little success, but development never stops in motor sport and the car was no longer an outright winner. The exercise had also been expensive – 'I would prefer to throw a veil over the financial side of things.' In 1966, no doubt with a tear in his eye, he sold CSX2001 to Pierre Landereau.

Landereau was a passionate member of both the motorcycle and car fraternities, and a biking buddy of former motorcycle champion turned F1 driver Jean-Pierre Beltoise, as well as a close friend of multiple Grand Prix winner Jacques Laffite, many of whose cars he collected. Landereau operated a specialist car dealership, Stand 14, located opposite Beltoise's Mille Milles operation on the RN20 near the Montlhéry circuit. He would also go on to become a veteran of 20 Paris-Dakar rallies, 13 of them on motorcycles.

One can imagine such a man having a lot of fun with CSX2001, though little is known of his time with the car other than it was presumably him who had it resprayed from its original colour of red to yellow. It was certainly that sunny hue by December 1967 when it was prominent in a photoshoot for the magazine *Salut les Copains*, featuring the enduring French rock and roll singer Johnny Hallyday. The bodywork remained

The first production Cobra

largely unchanged apart from the fact the complex Vincent bonnet had been superseded by a standard item with a simple scoop, not dissimilar to the one Hugus had fitted originally although it was longer and set further back on the nose. Gone too was the instantly recognisable roll bar and in its place a single centrally-mounted hoop, while the Vincent-inspired quick-lift jack brackets had been replaced by standard Cobra over-riders and nudge bars.

Rumour has it that the car suffered an engine fire while in Hallyday's care, causing him to abandon it in Paris and Landereau to recover it on a trailer. Whatever, at some stage its title passed to an André Pibaro of Bar-le-Duc but was still in storage at Landereau's garage when Hervé Arnone-Demoy of Casablanca took a liking to it. Pibaro refused to sell, but had heard of a Porsche 550RS in Morocco and said if Arnone-Demoy could secure it for him then perhaps a deal over the Cobra could be on after all. However, Pibaro also had Swiss sports car dealer Pierre de Sibenthal hunting for the Porsche and he pipped Arnone-Demoy to the post. Nevertheless, the story had a happy ending, with each man getting the car he wanted, though to seal his part of the bargain, Arnone-Demoy had to travel to

Part way through the 1965 season, Vincent removed CSX2001's controversial hardtop altogether, added some broad white stripes to the paintwork and a pair of racing mirrors to the front wings. Here he's seen tackling the Course de Côte de La Pommeraye.
Private collection

Vincent's final competition outing with CSX2001 was the 1965 Rallye de l'AGACI, an event he had won the previous year with fellow Frenchman Franck Ruata. This time their trusty steed failed to complete the event, melting its spark plugs here at Reims.
Private collection

The first production Cobra

Switzerland with the appropriate level of cash (money accrued from the sale of an MGA, Austin-Healey 3000 and Corvette), which he secreted in his shoes!

Arnone-Demoy disliked the state of the body, so had it refurbished and painted orange – 'it was an "in" colour of the time.' He also replaced the modest bonnet scoop with one in 427-style and added an intake for the oil cooler. For two years he 'drove the car like crazy to the office, night clubs etc' before reluctantly advertising

● While in the care of Montlhéry-based garagiste Pierre Landereau, CSX2001 was loaned to the enduring French rock and roll singer Johnny Hallyday for a feature in the magazine *Salut les Copains*. Note the change from red to yellow and minor updates to the bodywork.
Private collection

it internationally, as he needed to fund a world tour. The global advertising failed, so he took the car back to Paris in the autumn of 1974 and ended up selling it to rural *garagiste* Bernard Afchain, who by coincidence lived a mere 10 miles from where Arnone-Demoy was staying.

Like Arnone-Demoy before him, Afchain was underwhelmed with both the condition of the body and its colour, so initiated further restoration. And it was during this latest round of refurbishment that a fundamental fact was revealed – namely, that first Arnone-Demoy and then Afchain had purchased the car under the impression it was chassis COX6010, the Cobra originally campaigned by Jean de Mortemart.

One can well imagine Afchain's surprise when stripping the car unearthed identification markings not for COX6010 but CSX2001. Suitably confused, he contacted Vincent and discovered that during 1965, when Jean Marie was competing with CSX2001, he additionally acquired both CSX2142 (the Ford France car frequently driven by Jo Schlesser) and COX6010. Both cars had been badly damaged – COX6010 had suffered a severely modified front end while CSX2142, the more highly developed of the two Cobras, had met its temporary doom on the Mont Ventoux hill-climb. Having salvaged the eight racing wheels and various other desirable spares from CSX2142, he redeployed much of COX6010 to repair CSX2142 and scrapped the remainder of the de Mortemart car – that is with the exception of its *carte gris* and foot box identity plate, as these solved a long-standing issue for him. In a nutshell, CSX2001 had arrived in Europe on Pennsylvania registration plates and never been road-registered in France. Now, having a complete registration for a car that no longer existed (COX6010) and a complete car with no registration (CSX2001) he had simply attached COX6010's chassis tag and number plates to CSX2001. *Voilà* – problem solved!

Having officially re-established its identity, Afchain re-assembled CSX2001, finished it in its original red livery and retained it until selling to Swiss collector Dominik Ellenreider in 2000. Ellenreider treated it to still further sympathetic restoration, during which

Hervé Arnone-Demoy treated CSX2001 to a spell in the sunny climes of Morocco, where he changed the livery from yellow to orange, a fashionable colour at the time, and 'drove the car like crazy to the office, night clubs etc'.
Private collection

The first production Cobra

- Orange may have been the 'in' colour in Morocco, but it was not to Bernard Afchain's liking and on his acquisition of CSX2001, he treated the car to a fair degree of restoration before returning it to its original red livery.
Private collection

- It was while rebuilding the car Afchain discovered that, to overcome its ongoing lack of French registration papers, Vincent had simply switched its identity to that of COX6010 – a Cobra he had also owned at one stage!
Private collection

it was repainted a light metallic green and largely returned to its Vincent competition specification with quick-lift jack brackets, and even auxiliary lights mounted between them and the uniquely positioned sidelights; just as Vincent had run the car in the Rallye de l'AGACI. For the first time, CSX2001 was equipped with a technically acceptable roll hoop complete with longitudinal bracing and a contemporary FIA Historic Passport was issued.

By late 2005, Ellenreider had decided to move the car on and it was offered for sale by the respected Zurich-based historic car dealer Lukas Hüni, and ultimately purchased by American collector Bruce Meyer from Hüni's stand at Rétromobile in Paris the following February. After contesting the Budapest-Prague rally

The first production Cobra

By the year 2000, CSX2001 was in the hands of Swiss collector Dominik Ellenreider. This prompted further restoration and another change of colour – this time to a light metallic green.
Private collection

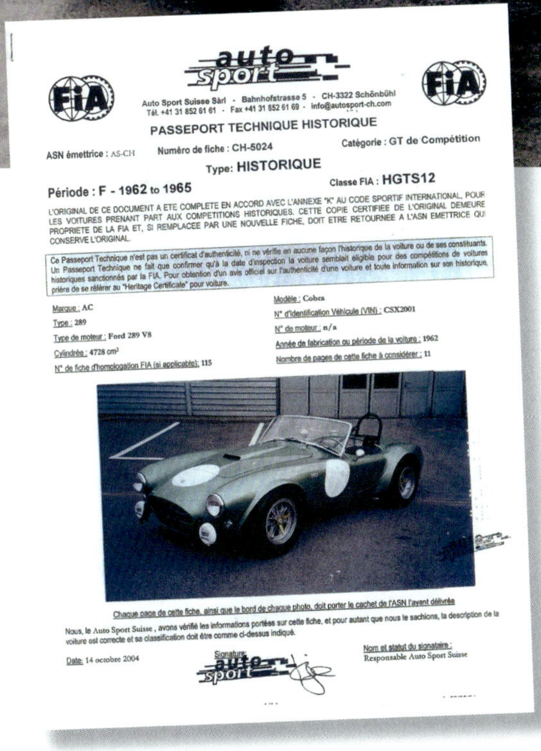

While Landereau, Arnone-Demoy and Afchain had biased the Cobra's specification to road use, Ellenreider went some way to returning CSX2001 to the racing set-up originated by Vincent and acquired an FIA Historic Passport for the car.
Private collection

with the car, Meyer exported it to his native California, where renowned Cobra guru Mike McCluskey was tasked with treating this well-preserved original-bodied racer to a sympathetic nut-and-bolt restoration.

Never a fan of green and having already owned two Cobras in red (CSX2001's original colour), Meyer had the car finished in his favourite hue – black. This stunningly presented member of the Cobra family now dwells in Meyer's private museum in Beverly Hills, which it shares with such equally historically important cars as the Porsche 935 K3 that won Le Mans outright in 1979, and four class winners from that incomparable annual 24-hour marathon – a Ferrari 250 GT SWB 'SEFAC' from the 1961 event, the 1965 Iso Bizzarrini A3/C, 1969 Porsche 910, and 2009 Corvette C6R.

The first production Cobra

CSX2001 in summary

Like all Bruce Meyer's wonderful collection of cars, the Cobra is these days immaculate, on the button and frequently used – it is also remarkably original. It ticks many boxes for him. Firstly there is the connection to its maker – Carroll Shelby was a personal friend. Then there is the link to Le Mans – Bruce's emotional attachment to the world's greatest long distance sports car race is self-evident from the cars that he owns.

Although CSX2001 eventually failed to contest Le Mans in 1964, it did acquit itself well at the Test Weekend. It was also the only Shelby roadster to take part in the extraordinarily tough Tour de France and the only privately entered leaf spring example to make an indelible mark on the European racing scene. It is without question one of the most important links in the entire Cobra chain.

- Bruce Meyer purchased CSX2001 off Lukas Hüni's stand at Rétromobile, Paris in 2006. Behind the still green Cobra can be seen former owners Bernard Afchain, Hervé Arnone-Demoy and Jean Marie Vincent.
Bruce Meyer collection

- Back to its winning ways - CSX2001 retired from racing many years ago, but is still collecting awards. Here it is pictured on the rostrum at The Quail, Monterey, in 2008, where the Cobra won both 'Best of Show' and the 'Postwar Competition' class.
Bruce Meyer collection

Lloyd Casner

Casner's involvement in the history of 2001 was short-lived but fundamentally important for, as we have seen, it was he that made it possible for Jean Marie Vincent to realise his dream of owning a Cobra and, as a result, become the only private entrant to so extensively compete with a leaf spring Cobra in Europe in period.

Like Vincent, Casner was an airline pilot by profession. He was also a racing enthusiast and, inspired by the introduction of the 'Birdcage' Maserati, created the team Camoradi (**Ca**sner **Mo**tor **Ra**cing **Di**vision) International in order to contest the Le Mans 24 hour race. The cars were supplied and prepared by Maserati and the team funded by Casner courtesy of sponsorship from such major organisations as Goodyear, Shell/BP, Exide, Champion, Koni, Dow Chemicals and Guest Airways. Camoradi was arguably America's first industry-backed international motor racing team.

No less than three Birdcages were entered for the 1960 Le Mans race, but none lasted the distance. In fact Camoradi 'works' Maseratis led every World Sports Car Championship race during that season, but the sole victory achieved was courtesy of Stirling Moss and Dan Gurney in the Nürburgring 1,000km event. The team won the same race the following year – this time with Masten Gregory and Casner himself sharing the honours. Other top drivers to represent the team included Jo Bonnier and one Carroll Shelby, who won a USAC race at Riverside for the equipe in 1960.

Camoradi also ran an ex-Behra Porsche (1960) and a Cooper-Climax (1961) in Formula One and Casner himself contested one non-championship F1 event – the 1961 Glover Trophy at Goodwood. Casner's nickname was 'Lucky', but the lady of that ilk was sadly not at his side when he was driving a Maserati Tipo 151 for the French distributor in the 1965 Le Mans Trial. A mechanical failure caused the car to crash and Casner was killed, aged just 36.

● Lloyd 'Lucky' Casner created the racing team Camoradi International in order to contest the Le Mans 24 Hours with the 'Birdcage' Maserati. Three were entered for the 1960 event, though none made it to the finish. Here we see the entry of Casner and Jim Jeffords.
Ferret Fotographics & LAT Images

The first production Cobra

Ed Hugus

Most people were blissfully unaware of it at the time, but without Ed Hugus Project Cobra would almost certainly never have got off the ground. Before the deal with Ford was fully in place, the money owed to AC had to come from another source. It should have been Shelby himself, but he did not have the funds and it was his friend Hugus that reputedly picked up the tab.

The two men were as alike as they were different. Both had survived World War II (Hugus was a paratrooper with a bad knee injury to show for it) and both were experienced racing drivers. However, they greatly differed in their demeanour – Hugus was a soft-spoken, modest individual – and, unlike Shelby at that stage, had many years of success in the automotive world behind him. He had established the second Ferrari dealership in the US and his European Cars concern was the go-to East coast supplier for a variety of different marques of car from across the pond.

It is worth diverting for a moment to Hugus's racing achievements, as they include several fascinating claims to fame. For example, he may well hold the record for the greatest number of Le Mans starts by an American driver (10) as he contested every event from 1956 to 1965 inclusive. Also it was he, not Shelby American, who jointly gave the Cobra its first taste of Le Mans, as he entered CSX2142 to drive with Peter Jopp in the 1963 event alongside CS2131 (better known by its registration plate 39 PH) which AC Cars was running for Peter Bolton and Ninian Sanderson. Unfortunately, the Hugus car developed such a serious oil leak that it was disqualified. CS2131 on the other hand finished an impressive seventh overall and won its class.

The most intriguing fact, though, is that Hugus may have actually won the 1965 Le Mans race but, unlikely as it may seem, history has so far been unable to confirm it. What is indisputable is that he was the reserve driver of the winning Ferrari 250LM from the North American Racing Team. The story goes that when Masten Gregory ended a stint prematurely and Jochen Rindt was nowhere to be found, Hugus stepped into the breach and piloted the car for the next two hours. The tale did not surface until after Hugus had passed away. If it is true and had been made public during the race, the team would have been disqualified, as Rindt would have been regarded as replaced and therefore not allowed to drive the car again, which he did. With all three drivers long since departed for the race track in the sky, the truth may never be known.

● Hugus was among the first to run a Cobra at Le Mans when he contested the 1963 event in CSX2142 with Englishman Peter Jopp.
The Revs Institute for Automotive Research/ Albert Bochroch & LAT Images

Photo gallery

Studio photography by Peter Harholdt

The first production Cobra

- Despite a full and fascinating life, CSX2001 remains remarkably original, but has never looked more purposeful than it does in its current black livery. Note the early oblong bonnet badge as fitted to the car from birth.

● McCluskey's nut-and-bolt restoration will withstand any amount of close inspection. Here we see the relatively modest bonnet scoop (above left), the rear brake caliper (above) and the front brake scoops and quick-lift jack brackets (left).

These detail images reveal a front corner with leaf spring, damper, brake rotor and caliper (above), the cockpit with functional facia and twin rear-view mirrors (above right), and brace for the roll bar and driver's harness (right).

- Potent cars can be demanding beasts and CSX2001 has plenty of auxiliary gauges and switches (left) to keep the driver busy. The car was born with worm-and-sector steering and a flat wheel; the period conversion to rack-and-pinion required the change to a dished wheel (above).

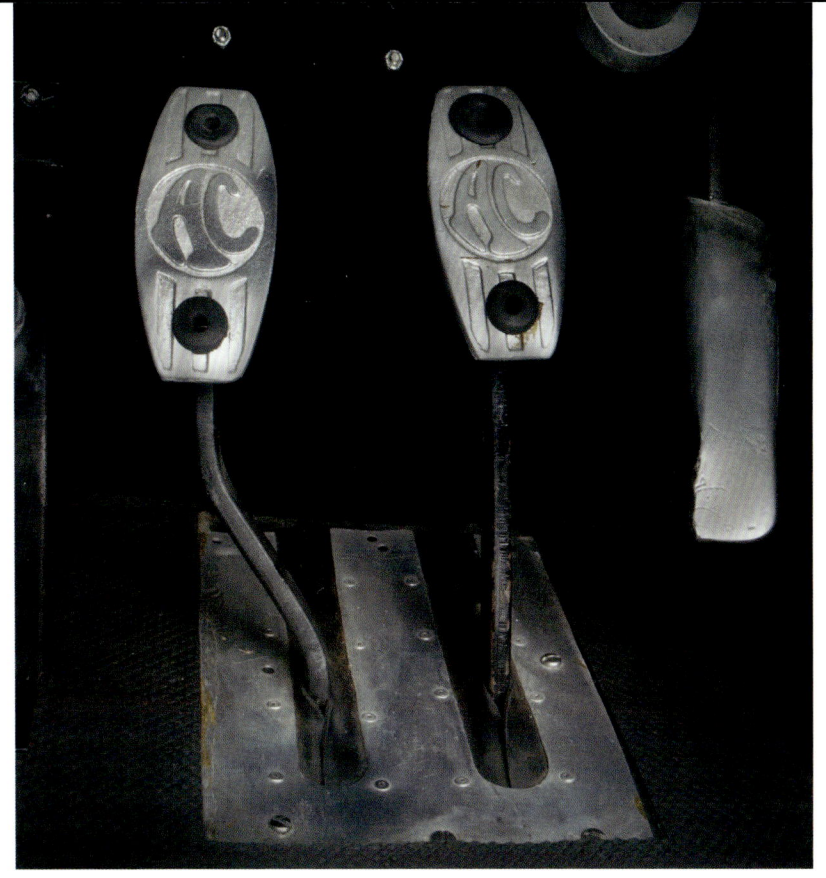

The cast pedals (above) are a reminder of the Cobra's heritage, as is the unmistakable signature (above right) adorning the lid of the glovebox. Under the bonnet (right) nestles the suitably tuned 289 V8 fed by a quartet of twin-choke Weber carburettors.

Next spread This doyen of Cobras looks good from any angle. Here we get a great view of the meaty Halibrand wheels, side exhaust, competition fuel filler, and quick-lift jack brackets. Everything combines to make it look mighty fast even when it is stationary.

Part 4
CSX2002

Thanks to the immaculate restoration carried out by Geoff Howard back in the 1970s, CSX2002 is nowadays presented exactly as it raced at Sebring in 1963, right down to the competition numbers and sponsors' decals.
Simon Clay

Nowadays, motor sport teams rely on computers to ensure components are sufficiently durable for the job in hand. Back in the early 1960s, testing at racing speeds was the only sure-fire indicator, and the Shelby team had precious little time for that before committing CSX2002 to its memorable showdown with Chevrolet's equally new Sting Rays at Riverside in October 1962. No doubt the failure of the car's rear hub while holding a commanding lead would have been a bitter blow to all concerned, but the speed of the car prior to that was a major statement in itself.

These days, the car is resplendent in the exact livery of its inclusion in the five-car Cobra assault on the 1963 Sebring 12 Hours. Though this was another non-finish for CSX2002, by the time it was sold to Ford Canada for use by Comstock Racing a few months later it had contributed a great deal to the development of the breed and been campaigned by Dan Gurney, Bill Krause, Dave MacDonald and Ken Miles – some of the very best drivers of the day. It then did much to enhance the Canadian racing scene of the 1960s and 1970s before being treated to a well-earned restoration and comfortable retirement.

Chapter 6
The first works racing Cobra

As CSX2001 was assembled by Ed Hugus's operation, CSX2002 has the distinction of being the first production specification Cobra to be readied for use by Shelby American itself.

Rather than then being allocated to one of the Ford dealers so desperate to inject some excitement into their showrooms, it was selected to be the company's first works race car. This was a brave but inevitable move – Shelby's Cobra dream was founded on creating a winning vehicle and he couldn't wait to get one on track. Moreover, nobody was more aware of Ford's 'win on Sunday, sell on Monday' philosophy, and therefore saw success in motor sport as the quickest and surest way of persuading the Blue Oval to fully commit to his cause.

Shelby decided the debut would be at the *Los Angeles Times* Grand Prix meeting at Riverside on 13 October 1962. The race was a three-hour contest for production sports cars and the driver was 29-year-old Californian Bill Krause, who had made his name in the mid-1950s at the wheel of a D-type Jaguar and more recently in a Birdcage Maserati.

Phil Remington set about preparing the mount for a full assault on the latest version of Ford's old nemesis, the Chevrolet Corvette – of which four were entered. In common with the new fully independently-sprung Sting Rays that it would be pitched against, the Cobra was not yet homologated, so would run with 'XP' for Experimental on its flanks. Modifications to the Cobra included: a modest bonnet scoop, behind which sat no less than five sets of louvres to help reduce air pressure and aid cooling; a baffled sump; racing exhausts exiting just ahead of the rear wheels; a single-hoop roll bar; and Perspex aero-screen.

Following a Le Mans-type start, the race was headed by Dave MacDonald in the first of the Sting Rays but it wasn't long before Krause was hot on his heels. He then assumed the lead on lap nine and was holding it comfortably when, five circuits later, the offside rear hub broke and the wheel parted company. Doug Hooper won in his Mickey Thompson-entered Corvette but, like the Cobra, the other Sting Rays of MacDonald, Grant and Bondurant all retired. It was a shame the Cobra was denied a fairy-tale maiden victory, but no great surprise bearing in mind the Shelby team's lack of time to prepare and test what was, after all, a completely new race car. More to the point, it was obvious to all that the Cobra had the legs on its arch rival. The future looked promising.

With uprated hubs and further tweaks installed, the team headed to the Bahamas for the popular Nassau Speed Week series of races. History relates that three events were contested. Krause was running second in the first qualifying race behind a Ferrari GTO when the tie-rod end broke and he was pitched into the bushes. A win was looking very realistic in the Tourist Trophy event when the car ran out of fuel, while the Governor's Trophy race resulted in another non-finish. It was not the sort of showing Shelby needed or envisaged, and no doubt contributed to Krause vacating the Ford fold to drive for Chevrolet.

Shelby's solution was to sign up Dave MacDonald and Ken Miles, both of whose names would quickly become synonymous with the Cobra brand. Much

The second outing for works racer CSX2002 was at the 1962 Nassau Speed Week. Wearing no. 98, it is seen here with Bill Krause on board. Alongside is CSX2011, the first racing Cobra sold to the public, bought and campaigned by John Everly.
The Henry Ford/Dave Friedman

The first works racing Cobra

- For five glorious laps, Bill Krause looked as though he was going to give CSX2002 victory in its maiden race, but it was ultimately sidelined by a broken rear hub. However, the message was still emphatic – Shelby's baby was quicker than Chevrolet's new Corvette.
The Henry Ford/Dave Friedman

time had also been invested in the specification of the race cars, the main focus of which concerned the model's transverse leaf suspension for which countless combinations of spring lengths and stiffness, settings for the new Koni dampers, and different weights of anti-roll bars were investigated. The first race of the 1963 season was at Riverside on 3 February. CSX2002 was not present, but it was memorable for being the scene of the first-ever Cobra win, courtesy of MacDonald aboard chassis CSX2026.

Meanwhile, CSX2002 had been prepared as part of a three-car assault on the Daytona 3 Hours on 17 February. The meeting marked the model's first foray into international racing and also Dan Gurney's inaugural Cobra drive. Instead of the 260cu.in. cast-iron version of Ford's Windsor engine used by the team to date, the Cobras for Dave MacDonald and Skip Hudson were powered by the upcoming 289 cu.in.

variant, topped by a quartet of Weber carburettors. The unit initially fitted to CSX2002 for Gurney to drive was even more special, being one of the ultra-rare all-aluminium 260 units being developed for Ford's Indianapolis programme that had so far only done time on a dynamometer. The combination was clearly a risky strategy.

And so it proved to be, for there was drama for CXS2002 from the outset, with a core plug parting company just before the start. Somehow the team managed to swap the recalcitrant unit for a regular iron one in time for Gurney to join the race two laps down. Incredibly, he made up the handicap, but on the 48th lap, just when he seemed destined to take the lead, the replacement engine suffered terminal ignition failure and CSX2002's race was run. Poor Hudson suffered an exploding flywheel that crushed his ankle and trapped the steering column, causing the car to crash, but

The first works racing Cobra

Here we see Krause skilfully opposite-locking the Cobra in pursuit of MacDonald's flying Corvette. He overtook the Chevy on lap 9 and had built up a commanding lead by the time the hub let go.
The Henry Ford/Dave Friedman

Another fine view of Krause balancing the Cobra on the throttle. The 'XP' next to the competition number stood for 'Experimental' – like the Corvette, the Cobra was yet to be homologated for racing in such events.
The Henry Ford/Dave Friedman

MacDonald managed fourth place behind a pair of GTO Ferraris and a Corvette. Mixed fortunes, but to those present, including the men from Ford, the Cobra was showing potential, if not reliability.

Next up on CSX2002's calendar was an SCCA race through the car park of the stadium of the famous LA Dodgers baseball team. Despite the course being largely defined by straw bales, the event was well attended and therefore meaningful for Shelby when his cars romped home to a convincing win for MacDonald and second place for Miles in CSX2002.

So to the Sebring 12 Hours, for which no less than five Cobras were entered – four by Shelby American and one by Holman & Moody. This was to be the model's first crack at long distance racing and to quote Shelby after the event, 'everything that could go wrong or fall off, did!'

The mood had been very different beforehand.

The first works racing Cobra

Bill Krause

Bill Krause's father was involved in Midget racing and that's where the youngster started his driving career, winning a title in 1955. However, his mother had safety concerns about such open-wheel racing and, following a couple of accidents, his father purchased him a D-type Jaguar in time for the 1956 season. He won his first race starting from 13th place on the grid and never looked back.

During a memorable joust in the 1958 *Los Angeles Times* Grand Prix at Riverside, Krause finished third behind Chuck Daigh and Dan Gurney amid a field of F1, Indy and top SCCA contenders, causing Jean Behra, who had finished fourth, to suggest Krause was the 'best of all the drivers there'.

In 1959 he began driving Maseratis for the Brumby team, and won the 1960 *Los Angeles Times* Grand Prix at the wheel of a Birdcage ahead of such world-class talent as Stirling Moss and Dan Gurney in Lotus 19s. It was following a run of impressive results in Maseratis that he was hired by Shelby for the Cobra's all-important first race and, as recorded elsewhere, comfortably had the measure of MacDonald's Corvette before a rear hub let him down.

At the end of that season he was lured from the Shelby squad by Mickey Thompson with the promise of not only a Corvette drive but a crack at the Indy 500. Sadly for him, General Motors politics intervened and he only got to contest one meeting at the wheel of a works Corvette – Daytona in February 1963. He did attempt to qualify for the Indy 500, but withdrew his entry after the car doused his face in oil at 200mph.

Krause retired from the sport in 1966 following which he ran a Honda motorcycle dealership and car outlets for a variety of manufacturers.

● Bill Krause made his name in a D-type Jaguar provided by his father. His third place in the 1958 *Los Angeles Times* Grand Prix behind Chuck Daigh and Dan Gurney caused Jean Behra, who finished fourth, to suggest he was the 'best of all the drivers there'.
The Revs Institute for Automotive Research/William Hewitt

The first works racing Cobra

- In February 1963, CSX2002 was part of a three car assault in the Daytona 3 Hours. For this event it was piloted by Dan Gurney who, following problems, began the race two laps down yet still looked set to sweep into the lead when ignition failure cruelly halted his progress on lap 48.
Getty Images

Two of the Shelby cars were brand new, complete with soon-to-be-standard rack-and-pinion steering systems, while the other two, including CSX2002, were survivors from the Daytona race and still equipped with worm-and-sector set-ups. By now all were powered by notably uprated 289 engines. Their cylinder heads had been skimmed to give a compression ratio of 11:1, requiring the crowns of the stock aluminium pistons to be machined to prevent them kissing the valves. The gas flow within the inlet and exhaust ports was further improved and all internal parts balanced. As a result, output was now reputed to be up to 330bhp. Braking was aided by a pair of substantial ducts under the nose, while the wheel arches had been additionally flared to shroud wider Halibrand 'kidney bean' wheels in place of the standard wires. The brackets for the windscreen had been modified to increase the rake and therefore improve the cars' high speed aerodynamics. Unlike the bonnet first run on CSX2002 that had a modest scoop and no less than five small vents at the rear, the cars now featured a bigger scoop and two large rear vents, plus locks with external turn-buckles in place of those needing to be operated by fiddly T handles. Detail features included a pair of Raydyot rear view mirrors, a splash guard to protect the driver during fuel stops, an elastic strap to ensure the boot-lid didn't spring open in the heat of battle, quick-lift jack brackets front and rear, a lightweight driver's seat, stone guards protecting

The first works racing Cobra

- Following Daytona, Shelby entered a pair of team cars for the SCCA event at the stadium of the LA Dodgers baseball team. The course was Mickey Mouse but the competition strong. MacDonald won with Miles a close second in CSX2002. *The Henry Ford/Dave Friedman*

the headlights, and a gauze-covered front nudge hoop to protect the air intake and auxiliary lights required for the night stint.

The Shelby driver line-up was certainly impressive and comprised Phil Hill, Dan Gurney, Dave MacDonald, Glenn 'Fireball' Roberts, Lew Spencer and the redoubtable Ken Miles. Ultimately though, these drivers were swapped ad nauseam in an attempt to keep the cars going against the odds, and in the end only the Hill car (also driven by Miles and Spencer) was in contention, finishing 11th overall and first in class. CSX2002 was ascribed competition No.16 and assigned to Ken Miles and Lew Spencer to drive, however, Spencer never even got behind the wheel as oil pump failure was followed by a broken rocker before a fractured steering arm terminated the car's best-forgotten outing.

By this time the Cobras had proved they were more than a match for all rivals when running and it was only a matter of time before the reliability issues that were letting them down in longer events would be conquered. Victories, or at least podium finishes, in shorter SCCA races were now expected rather than just hoped-for. And this was certainly the pattern for CSX2002's final two meetings as a works racer, with Dave MacDonald taking it to an overall win at Tucson on 31 March and second place at Del Mar on 28 April. The pace of development at Shelby American was rising rapidly and it was time for CSX2002 to pass the baton to new examples of the breed, so in May 1963 it was sold to Ford of Canada for use by Comstock Racing.

Comstock was, and still is, a major Toronto-based engineering construction company, established by the Rathgeb family and for many years run by Charles 'Chuck' Rathgeb Jnr. A former member of the Royal Canadian Mounted Police and Royal Canadian Navy, he was a keen and able sportsman who hit upon motor sport by chance, and ended up founding

The first works racing Cobra

Five Cobras were entered for the 1963 Sebring 12 Hours, the team's first attempt at long distance racing. It was not a success, with Shelby saying 'everything that could go wrong or fall off did'! CSX2002 (no.16) failed to finish.
The Revs Institute for Automotive Research/Albert Bochroch

CSX2002's last race as a works car was in an SCCA Divisional event at Del Mar, California. The drive was entrusted to Dave MacDonald. Ever quick, on this occasion he had to give best to the Corvette of Paul Reinhart.
The Henry Ford/Dave Friedman

Dan Gurney

Daniel Sexton Gurney may only have driven CSX2002 once but, as we have seen, he looked on course to win with it until ignition failure intervened. However, this doyen of American motor sport contributed a great deal to the overall Cobra racing programme. Of particular note was that outright victory in the 1963 Bridgehampton 500km event, which was not only the first major win for the Shelby team, but the first FIA race victory ever recorded by an American driver in an American car, and the first time a Ford engine had powered an FIA winner – it was a big deal all round!

In addition to piloting Cobra roadsters at Daytona, Sebring and Riverside in 1963, Gurney brought home a GT class victory for the roadster at the 1964 Targa Florio in Sicily and in the same year raced the Daytona Cobra Coupes at Le Mans, Reims and Goodwood, taking another two GT class victories (at Le Mans and Goodwood).

Gurney is also the only man to score maiden Grand Prix victories for three different manufacturers – Porsche, Brabham and his own All American Racers. In 1971 he invented the Gurney Flap (a small tab that projects upwards from the trailing edge of a racing car rear wing to increase downforce), which has been used in racing and aviation ever since. The bump that Ford put into the roof of the GT40 to accommodate the helmet atop Dan's lanky 6ft. 3in. frame was christened the 'Gurney Bubble'. Last but not least, he started the tradition of spraying rather than just drinking champagne on the victory podium. This occurred after he and AJ Foyt won Le Mans for Ford in 1967, and has since been emulated by winners everywhere.

● Dan Gurney only drove CSX2002 once – in the Daytona 3 Hours – but contributed an enormous amount to the Cobra programme. His outright victory in the 1963 Bridgehampton 500km was a massive coup for both Shelby and Ford.
The Revs Institute for Automotive Research/ Karl Ludvigsen & Albert Bochroch

The first works racing Cobra

Comstock Racing, Canada's first truly professional racing organisation. For the 1963 season he formed a partnership with Ford, which was seeking dominance in the North American market in any and every way it could. A deal was struck whereby Ford supplied the cars, engines and parts and Comstock provided the premises, mechanics and drivers.

On acquisition, CSX2002 was re-liveried in the Comstock colours of white with green stripes and allocated the competition number 54 and, along with other examples of the latest Comstock fleet, was proudly displayed at the Toronto Auto Show. It was entrusted for the 1963 season to Eppie Wietzes, who had previously successfully campaigned a Sunbeam Alpine in Canadian local and national events with support from Norman & Wietzes, the garage business in which his father Jan was a partner. Between June and the end of September 1963, Wietzes contested at least 11 events as follows:

Date	Event	Result
1 June	Players 200 Mosport	10th
15 June	GVCC Mosport	4th
30 June	USRRC – GT Watkins Glen	DNF
13 July	LASC Harewood	DNF
27 July	OLCC Mosport	1st
27 July	OLCC Mosport	1st
7 September	Indian Summer Mosport	3rd
7 September	Indian Summer Mosport	1st
15 September	MMGCC St-Eugène IV	3rd
15 September	MMGCC St-Eugène IV	3rd
28 September	GP Canada Mosport	6th (1st in class)

As can be seen, his victories all occurred at Mosport (the name is a contraction of the words motor and

● When Comstock Racing was loaned CSX2002, the team re-liveried the car and entrusted it to Eppie Wietzes. He did them proud – especially at the 1963 Canadian Grand Prix meeting, where he pipped none other than Ken Miles to a class win.
Klemantaski Collection/ Jack Whorwood

The First Three Shelby Cobras | 99

The first works racing Cobra

Dave MacDonald

Dave MacDonald drove each brand of Shelby Cobra – the roadster, Daytona Cobra Coupe and King Cobra (the Ford-powered mid-engined Cooper that Shelby also entered in US events in 1963 and 1964). MacDonald's extraordinary record of achievements include the following:

  First 260 roadster victory –
  2/3 February 1963, Riverside Raceway
  First 289 roadster victory –
  3/4 March 1963, Dodger Stadium
  First King Cobra victory –
  13 October 1963, Riverside Raceway
  First Daytona Cobra Coupe GT class victory –
  21 March 1964, Sebring

Carroll Shelby made his thoughts on MacDonald's driving abundantly clear in a 2008 interview with *Hot Rod* magazine: 'Dave MacDonald probably had more raw talent than any other race driver I ever saw.'

MacDonald first took to the tracks in 1956 driving a Corvette on Southern California drag strips. Still in Corvettes he switched to road racing in 1960 and was driving the latest version of the Chevrolet in the same race that Bill Krause debuted the Cobra at Riverside in October 1962. It was when Krause was offered a Corvette deal by Mickey Thompson that MacDonald joined the Shelby fold, for whom he logged some nine victories during the 1963 and 1964 seasons.

His racing career spanned eight years, during which he competed in 118 races, winning no less than 52 of them. There can be little doubt that many

● Dave MacDonald, pictured aboard a Corvette at Riverside in 1962 before he switched to the Shelby team. He went on to achieve numerous wins in a variety of Cobras.
The Revs Institute for Automotive Research/ William Hewitt & The Henry Ford/Dave Friedman

more triumphs would have followed had he not died following a fiery crash in the 1964 Indianapolis 500 in a Thompson-Ford – an incident that also cost the life of Eddie Sachs and marked the first occasion the famous race had to be stopped because of an accident. MacDonald was just 27 years old.

The first works racing Cobra

● Jean Ouellet bought CSX2002 to take his racing to the next level. Campaigning in the yellow of the Rimouski Racing Team, he notched up notable finishes at Mont-Tremblant and Mosport, earning the title of 'the most promising and popular driver in Quebec'.
Wilfrid Ouellet

sport), the international circuit located just north of Bowmanville, Ontario, that was the scene of 14 Canadian Grands Prix as well as epic Can-Am battles between 1966 and 1987. However, the one we imagine he will never forget will be that last one, played out on the international stage of his home Grand Prix (though Dutch by birth he had become a Canadian citizen). The top-class field included such big names as Graham Hill, John Surtees, Pedro Rodriguez, Lorenzo Bandini and Frank Gardner. For this event Wietzes also had an illustrious team-mate in the form of Ken Miles, who was on loan to Comstock from Shelby, together with the works racer CSX2129 that was resprayed in Comstock colours especially for the occasion.

The 100-lap race was won by Rodriguez in a Ferrari 250 P ahead of Graham Hill aboard a Lotus 23B, but the sometimes hair-raising duel that had the 24,000-strong crowd on their collective feet was that between Wietzes

The first works racing Cobra

Eppie Wietzes

Egbert 'Eppie' Wietzes was born in Assen, Holland in 1938 and was just 12 when his family emigrated to Canada. His racing career began in 1958 in a Morris Minor backed by Norman & Wietzes, the garage concern in which his father Jan was a partner. For the 1962 season he switched to a Sunbeam Alpine in which he achieved sufficient success to catch the eye of Comstock Racing, who entrusted him with their ex-works Cobra CSX2002 for the 1963 season.

Having proved more than up to the task, including beating the so-often-invincible Ken Miles to the line at the Canadian Grand Prix meeting, Wietzes continued to represent the Ford-backed Toronto-based team for the next three years; first at the wheel of a Shelby Mustang GT350 and then the GT40 P/1037.

Wietzes competed in the Canadian Grands Prix of 1967 at the wheel of a Lotus-Ford and 1974 in a Brabham-Ford, while at the 1973 meeting he became the first person to drive an F1 safety car, taking a Porsche 914 course vehicle on track following a collision between Jody Scheckter and François Cevert. He later enjoyed success in Formula 5000 and won the 1981 Trans-Am Series driving a Chevy Corvette before hanging up his helmet in 1987.

● Dutch-born Eppie Wietzes's long and successful racing career began in 1958 with a Morris Minor and included winning the 1981 Trans-Am Series with a Corvette. Here he is seen in a Formula 1 Lotus 49 and the Comstock GT40 (P/1037), symbolically overtaking a Cobra at Sebring in 1966.
The Revs Institute for Automotive Research/ Karl Ludvigsen & Albert Bochroch

Exceptional Cars

and Miles. It went right down to the chequered flag with Wietzes eventually crossing the line first to finish sixth overall and winner of the GT class.

Following a promising season, Comstock decided to shuffle its racing pack and offer CSX2002 for sale via the *Canadian Track & Traffic* publication. The advert was spotted by privateer racer Jean Ouellet of Rimouski who had achieved impressive results at the airfield circuit of St-Eugène during 1963 at the wheel of a flame-red 1959 Corvette, but had aspirations to climb the racing tree and felt the Cobra was perfect for his next assault. A cheque for $8,000 duly changed hands, and he ran the Cobra for the next two seasons, sporting competition number 83 and notching up some notable finishes.

The Ouellet racing effort was very much a family affair, with Jean supported at the meetings by his wife and two brothers. His mechanic was Rimouski Ford employee Hermel Lavoie, who etched his name in a different set of record books by preparing and supporting Mylène Paquette's solo boat crossing of the Atlantic in 2013. Jean Ouellet's major results in CSX2002 were as follows:

2 August (1964)	Mont-Tremblant	3rd
2 August	Mont-Tremblant	2nd
23 August	Mont-Tremblant	1st
5 September	Mosport	1st
13 September	Mont-Tremblant	7th
13 September	Mont-Tremblant	1st
18 October	Mont-Tremblant	7th
18 October	Mont-Tremblant	3rd
29 May (1965)	Mont-Tremblant	2nd
4 July	Labatt 50 Mont-Tremblant	7th
8 August	Mont-Tremblant	3rd
25 September	GP Canada Mosport	DNF
25 September	GP Mosport	26th

The 1964 achievements netted him the title of 'the most promising and popular driver in Quebec' while those over the two seasons won him a drive in the brand-new Ford GT40 (P/1000 – the first production example) loaned to Comstock in time for Ouellet and Bob McLean to contest the Sebring 12 Hours in March 1966. The future looked so promising, but poor McLean suffered a horrific accident during the race from which he was fatally injured. This had so profound an effect on Ouellet that he never competed again, and a burgeoning career was curtailed prematurely.

Still liveried in the yellow of the Rimouski Racing Team, CSX2002 was then sold to Jean Paul Ostiguy, a doctor from Montreal, who sometimes shared the car with André Samson. Their results include:

| 11 June (1967) | Mont-Tremblant | 10th | Ostiguy |
| 30 July | Mont-Tremblant | Not known | Ostiguy |

Jean Ouellet began his competition career with rallies and hill-climbs close to his home in Rimouski, Quebec, so felt at home running the Cobra in such types of event. Here he tackles 'La Montée de L'Hôpital', Gaspé, Quebec. *Robert Charbonneau*

The first works racing Cobra

Jean Ouellet

Jean Ouellet's prowess behind the wheel of CSX2002 led to him sharing the Comstock-run GT40 P/1000 with Bob McLean in the 1966 Sebring 12 Hours. The fatal accident that befell McLean so affected Ouellet that he never raced again.
Private collection

Jean's father Wilfrid operated a General Motors franchise in Quebec on the shores of the St Lawrence River, so Ouellet Junior was surrounded by cars from birth. He and his friend Marius Amiot began their competition careers courtesy of the local rallies and hill-climbs before progressing to circuit racing.

The deal to acquire Cobra CSX2002 was done in time for him to take delivery at the final meeting of the season at St Eugène, Ontario. Used to driving his Corvette to and from meetings, it had never occurred to him that the full-race Cobra was not street-legal, so he had to dip further into his pocket and purchase the trailer it had arrived on in order to get home.

With the car still in Comstock colours and wearing Wietzes's competition number 54, Ouellet contested three races that day, winning two of them and taking class honours in the third. The meeting concerned was not only the last of the 1963 season but the last ever at St-Eugène, and for 1964 the region was to be treated to a fresh venue, Mont-Tremblant.

The new track, outside the town of St Jovite, came with sponsorship from the Canadian beer company Labatt and, thinking outside the box, Ouellet figured that running the Cobra in their corporate colour of gold might encourage them to back him too. Sadly this inspired ploy failed and the car was resprayed yellow, the livery of the Rimouski Racing Team Ouellet formed with Marius Amiot.

So began the two years of success chronicled earlier, and one can only speculate as to what racing heights Ouellet might have scaled had his GT40 drive at Sebring ended more happily.

'Ouellet took delivery of CSX2002 at a race meeting. It never occurred to him that a full-race Cobra was not street-legal.'

The first works racing Cobra

• Records suggest that the Canadian Michel Tremblay was the last person to race CSX2002 in period, using it for a handful of circuit races and drag events, and it appears to have been him who resprayed the car from yellow to orange.
Private collection

27 August	GP Mosport	Not known	Samson
2 June (1968)	USRRC St Jovite	14th	Samson

The trail of CSX2002 then cools for a while, although the car seems to have remained in Canada well into the 1970s. Its next keeper is believed to have been Guy Lafleur of Quebec who then passed it on to a Michel Tremblay (though not the famous Montrealer novelist and playwright of the same name), who is on record as competing with the car at Mont-Tremblant in June 1969 – photos of the Cobra show that, like Ouellet before him, Tremblay had the mechanical support of Hermel Lavoie.

At some stage CSX2002 was re-painted orange, as it was finished in this colour when unearthed in a very dishevelled and damaged state in Boston, USA in September 1977. At this point it was purchased by Michael Shoen, the man who subsequently penned the respected book *The Cobra-Ferrari Wars: 1963-1965* and at one stage also owned the Daytona Cobra Coupe CSX2299 – the example with the most extensive racing history, which these days forms part of the amazing Larry Miller Collection. It is Shoen who must take the credit, not only for saving CSX2002 from possible extinction, but funding its return to as, or better than, new condition, in exactly the guise in which it wore competition no.16 at Sebring in 1963.

He entrusted the restoration to Geoff Howard of Danbury, Connecticut, who at the time was a commercial artist by day and Cobra refurbisher by night. However, on seeing what was required to bring CSX2002 up to the standard of his previous restorations, he put his art to one side and founded Accurate Restorations in order to work on the project full-time, which he did for the next two years. Said Howard: 'The car was together and running, but everything was wrong. The front of the chassis was an inch higher on the nearside than the offside. It had obviously taken a big hit there, and the original aluminium wing had been replaced with a glass-fibre one. Extra-large wheel arch flares had been pop-riveted on and there was filler everywhere. Half the nose was missing, as was the area under the boot. However, it still had its original works brake scoops, bonnet louvres, steering wheel, and Halibrand kidney bean wheels.'

The damaged chassis was straightened and painstakingly sleeved, the front suspension tower was rebuilt, the nose was replaced and body dents beaten out and new metal added where required. As the interior was effectively missing, new seats were made and trimmed from scratch. A fresh five-bolt HiPo engine was machined by Bob Sharp Racing (think Paul Newman and Nissan) and the unit lovingly assembled by Howard. Once sorted, the Cobra was resprayed in its original shade of red and, calling on his artistic skills, Howard even crafted perfect replicas of the Sebring decals and race numbers. The only departure from the Sebring specification requested by Shoen was the installation of an (easily removable) Austin-based rack-and-pinion steering system that was bolted onto the rear of the front suspension tower. $40,000 and 2,800 hours of hard labour later, CSX2002 was back to its former glory.

In the early 1980s, the Cobra was raced at Riverside by none other than Bill Krause, the man who had driven

The first works racing Cobra

it in its debut race at the very same Californian track, some 20 years earlier. Now aged 47, he once again led the pack until this time being black-flagged for a technical infringement.

Shoen retained CSX2002 for 22 years before placing it in the RM Sotheby's auction at Monterey in 1999, when it was purchased for $418,000 by the Larry Miller Collection, where these days it has CSX2000 for company.

● This is how down-at-heel CSX2002 looked by the time it was rescued by Michael Shoen in 1977. It took the 'Cobra Doctor' Geoff Howard 2,800 hours of expert craftsmanship to restore the car to its former glory.
Private collection

Thanks to Michael Shoen's investment and ● Geoff Howard's restoration skills, this is how CSX2002 looks today – exactly as it did prior to the 1963 Sebring 12 Hours. It nowadays forms part of the Larry Miller Collection.
Private collection

CSX2002 in summary

The life of a works race car is short and sweet. While it is competitive it receives the full gamut of everybody's attention – plus love and affection when it wins and vitriol when it doesn't. For a few weeks of 1962 CSX2002 was the total focus of Shelby's dream, the race car around which the Cobra's competition future was founded. The sight of it comfortably heading the field in its first race will doubtless forever live with those that witnessed it.

After a good innings with Shelby American and an impressive period in private hands it, like CSX2001, could so easily have been lost to obscurity had it not been for the dedication of a knowledgeable collector. In the case of CSX2002 it was Michael Shoen who saved it for posterity and it once again stands, right down to the merest detail, as it did the day it arrived for the 1963 Sebring 12 Hours.

The first works racing Cobra

Photo gallery

Studio photography by Simon Clay

• There is much to note about CSX2002 from this angle, not least: the brake scoops; gauze-covered nudge bar to protect the intake and auxiliary lights; the early 'Flat Head' badge on the nose; and the 'kidney bean' Halibrand wheels.

● Driver's-eye view as seen by Ken Miles at Sebring (left). Note the centrally placed Raydyot mirror and auxiliary switches on the facia. What a difference a number makes (above) – the '2002' marks this Cobra out as one of the most important of all.

Here we take a closer look at the early-style 'Flat Head' Cobra badge with blue background (above), the quick-release bonnet catches and additional central toggle fitted to all the Sebring cars (above right), and the competition fuel filler cap (right).

Facing page: Always a fine sight – a 289 V8 topped by a quartet of Weber carburettors; as raced at Sebring, CSX2002's unit would have delivered around 330bhp. This page: close-up views of the radiator expansion tank (above) and door mirror (right).

- The later works FIA racers featured wider bodies covering fatter wheels and tyres, but the general look and layout of the 289 competition cars remained much the same as CSX2002 throughout the model's stellar racing career.

The First Three Shelby Cobras

Part 5
Epilogue

A sight to excite any Cobra enthusiast – Carroll Shelby pictured with CSX2127, CSX2128 and CSX2129; team cars about to be transported to Pensacola, Florida for the first USRRC race of 1963.
Private collection

It is doubtful if Carroll Shelby made any long-term predictions for his 'sport car', but as a seasoned racing driver he would have been well aware how short the competition careers of most race cars are. History confirms that original Cobra production lasted some five years which, considering the car was founded on a nine-years old design, is pretty remarkable. More amazing still, though, is the fact that the brand has long since re-established itself at the top of many enthusiasts' wish lists, and continuation cars and replica products made by a host of independent suppliers continue to expand the history of the planet's speediest snake day by day.

The unashamed purpose of this book was to chart the lives and times of the first three Cobras – the platform on which one of the most famous automotive icons of all time was built. However, before signing off it would be a dereliction of duty not to at least briefly touch on the model's evolution from 260 to 289 to 427 (and 428) variants, and place a tiny bit of fat on the bones of the Daytona Cobra Coupe that brought Carroll Shelby's cars the international recognition he so ardently craved.

Chapter 7
Cobra later development

Describing the various versions of the Cobra has become a nightmare over time, as Shelby American was inconsistent with its model designations and some, especially British enthusiasts, have retrospectively adopted a Mark system which, to add to the confusion, means different things to different people. The safest way of identifying how the Cobra developed over time is by a combination of engine capacity and suspension, as follows:

CSX2000–c.2075

These cars were all powered by Ford's 260cu.in. version of its thin-walled Windsor V8 engine.

CSX/CS2075–2589
COB/COX6001–6062

This run of Cobras was all equipped with the larger variant of the Windsor unit, the 289cu.in. engine. Owners of road and race Cobras alike were quick to see the virtues of having a 289 engine in place of the 260, so very few of the original 75 cars still retain the smaller unit.

The first 51 or so cars featured the same leaf spring suspension and worm-and-sector steering as the 260-engined cars. The fundamental change from worm-and-sector to rack-and-pinion began with CSX2126 – this was accompanied by a revised front suspension tower and cast, as opposed to fabricated, uprights. There were many benefits to the steering update – it radically reduced the change in suspension geometry during cornering, was quicker and easier to service and stronger, so therefore less prone to breakage in the heat of competition.

The steering rack deployed was from the MGB and the steering column from the Volkswagen Beetle. As covered in the Technical Analysis (Chapter 3), the quickest way to distinguish between worm-and-sector and rack-and-pinion Cobras is via the steering wheel, as they are different and not interchangeable. With worm-and-sector Cobras came the option of a telescopically adjustable steering column, whereas rack-and-pinion columns were of a fixed length.

Shelby Daytona Cobra Coupe

The Cobra roadster was an ideal weapon for the typically tight curvy circuits on which the SCCA and USSRC championships were fought. But, as previously stated, Shelby's abiding aim was to beat Ferrari in Europe – especially at Le Mans where the Prancing Horse had been rampant since 1960 (in fact, since Shelby himself won for Aston Martin), and no American car had so far triumphed.

The first season of the roadster was sufficient to show that, no matter how much power you passed through the rear wheels, it was never going to catch a Ferrari 250 GTO down the Mulsanne straight, as the scarlet cars had a terminal speed advantage of 30mph due to their considerably more aerodynamic lines. When nobody was looking, Shelby ran the race cars with abnormally high rake on the windscreens but that could not make up for the car's fundamentally poor aerodynamics.

In time for the 1964 season, Shelby asked Peter

By winning its class at Reims, CSX2601 driven by Bob Bondurant and Jo Schlesser sealed GT victory in the 1965 World Sports Car Championship on July 4, Independence Day – wins do not come much sweeter than that for an American racing team.
The Revs Institute for Automotive Research/Eric della Faille

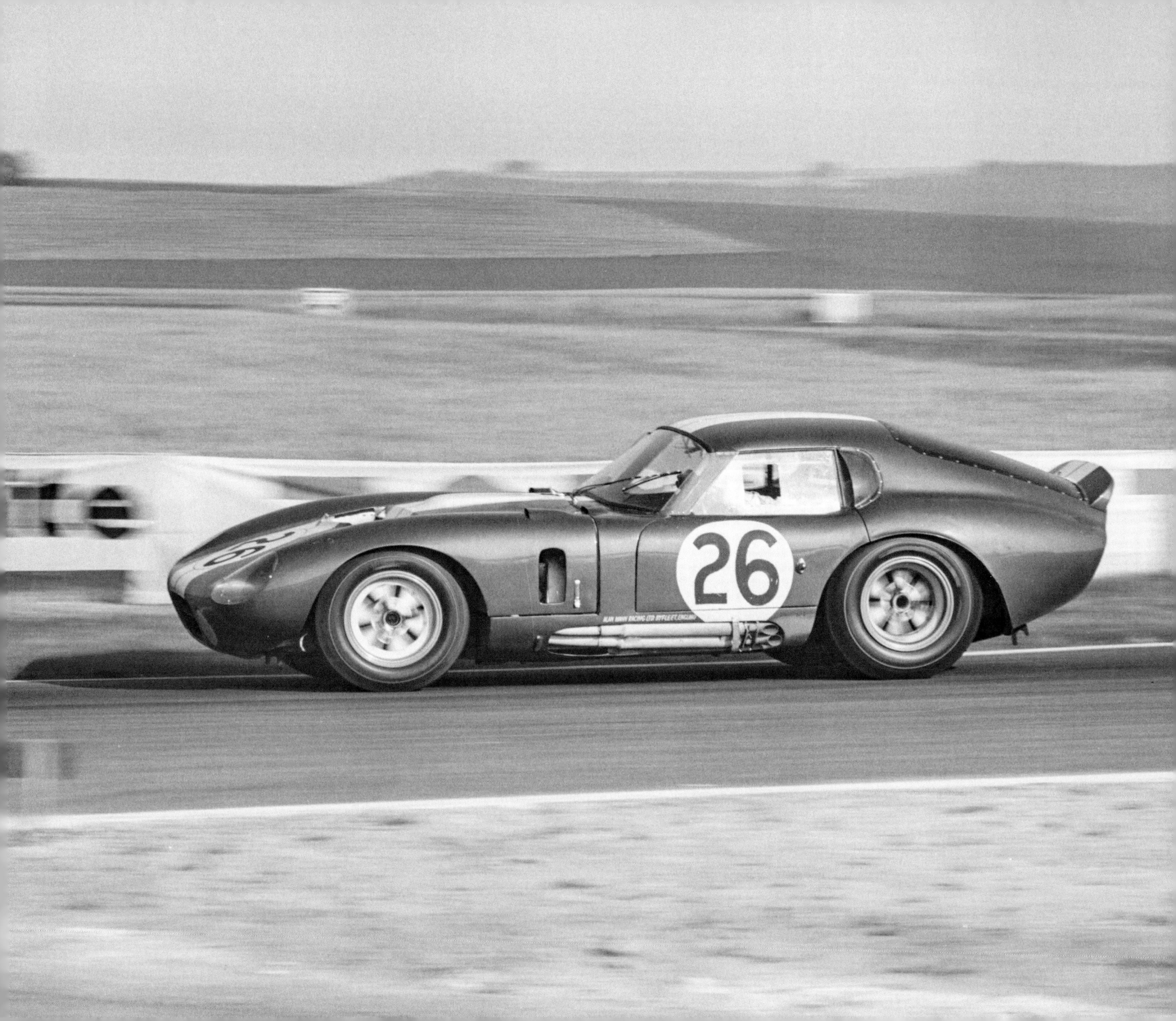

Cobra later development

- The prototype Cobra Coupe CSX2287 during initial tests at the Riverside Raceway. Note the forward-hinged front body section, which was also a feature of the Ken Miles 'Flip-Top' shown on page 120.
The Henry Ford/Dave Friedman

- Brock's confidence in his design was quickly vindicated and with a few amendments the Coupe proved capable of 190mph – way faster than any Cobra roadster had ever run.
The Henry Ford/Dave Friedman

Cobra later development

Brock to create a wind-cheating coupe. Having sketched his plan on the workshop floor, Brock proceeded to create a buck around the remains of the roadster CSX2014, on which the first alloy body was then hand-beaten.

Brock's colleagues were unconvinced by the somewhat ungainly design, so Shelby had it checked by an aviation expert who declared it would never work. But Brock, still only 27 years of age, stuck to his guns and in its first test at the Riverside Raceway, CSX2287 clocked 186mph, even though the steering became 'scarily light at that speed'. Thirty days later it was signed off by Miles, who had now achieved over 190mph in the car.

The coupe's first event was the 1964 Daytona Continental 2,000km. In the capable hands of Bob Holbert and Dave MacDonald, the car was a resounding four laps in the lead when it was suddenly sidelined by a bizarre

The Goodwood Revival meeting of 2015 was the first occasion on which all six Daytona Cobra Coupes had ever gathered together. In the foreground is CSX2601, the car that sealed championship honours for the team in 1965.
Private collection

The First Three Shelby Cobras

Cobra later development

- The 'Flip-Top' Cobra was created by master special builder Ken Miles, who shoehorned a 427 engine into the poor, unsuspecting 289 Cobra CSX2196. The conclusion was that a 427 version of the snake was a good idea, provided a new chassis was created!
Private collection

pit fire. Proven as the fastest GT racer of the time, the model was thereafter known as the Shelby Daytona Cobra Coupe.

Just six examples were built – the first by Brock at Shelby American and the other five by Carrozzeria Gransport in Modena, Italy. They were campaigned by Shelby in the USA and Alan Mann Racing in Europe, and were on course to win their class in the 1964 World Sports Car Championship when, in an extraordinary piece of gamesmanship even by his standards, Enzo Ferrari managed to persuade the FIA that points for the Monza race should not count, leaving championship victory to – yes, you have guessed it – Ferrari.

It was a close run competition again in 1965, but this time the Cobra Coupes prevailed, clinching Class III of the championship at Reims on 4 July – American Independence Day!

CSX/CSB3001–3360
COB/COX6101–6127

These cars all had coil spring suspension and were produced with either 289, 427 or 428 engines. Once reliable, the small-block Cobra ruled the roost in American domestic championships throughout the 1963 season. However, a drubbing at the annual end of year Nassau Speed Week courtesy of Chevrolet's prototype Grand Sport Corvettes showed what could happen should General Motors decide to make the necessary 100 cars to gain homologation for the production class. There were also rumours that Enzo Ferrari was attempting to achieve the same sleight of hand with the mid-engined 250 LM as he had managed when homologating the 250 GTO. Moreover, Shelby's ultimate goal was still to 'kick Ferrari's ass' on the

Cobra later development

international stage and it was now crystal clear he was never going to achieve that with the 289 Cobra.

Shelby 427

Various solutions were sought at making the roadster more competitive but with little in the way of budget to invest, the traditional American solution of adding cubic inches became the chosen route. Ken Miles's infamous 'Flip-Top' 427 prototype may have been almost impossible to drive, but nevertheless proved itself a lot quicker than the heavier Corvettes at the 1964 Nassau Speed Week before breaking. The case for more power was therefore accepted, as was that for markedly updating the Cobra's ageing leaf spring chassis.

The resulting, much stiffer, coil-sprung frame was unquestionably a step forward and improved both ride and handling. It was clothed in what, at first sight, looked like one of the existing FIA bodies, but was in fact both wider and longer and featured the enlarged air intake deemed necessary to keep 427 cubic inches of Ford ironmongery at an acceptable temperature. To either side of the new mouth there was an additional intake that fed in yet more air – to the engine compartment of the road versions, and the brakes on competition models.

For some, the dramatic presence of a 427 Cobra represents the pinnacle of the brand, and for quite a while it was certainly the fastest accelerating production car available in the US. Its race pedigree is less memorable. The minimum production required for homologation was 100, but by the time of the FIA inspection only 51 out-and-out competition cars had been delivered by AC so, with no prospect of gaining approval for the 1965 season, Shelby cancelled the balance of the order. In the end, just 23 of the 51 found buyers and the remainder were detuned, rebranded S/C (semi-competition) and offered as road cars alongside

The production 427 retained the basic form of the 289, but was wider and longer and featured a bigger central mouth sandwiched by a pair of additional intake grilles. It was America's fastest accelerating road car for quite some time.
The Henry Ford/Dave Friedman

The First Three Shelby Cobras | 121

Cobra later development

the standard version, of which 260 examples were made. Not quick to sell in the 1960s, genuine 427 S/Cs are now among the most sought after of all Cobra derivatives. Only one production 427 was ever raced by Shelby – CSX3002 – but a number of privateers ran and won with them well into the 1970s.

The irony of the programme is that General Motors never did homologate the Grand Sport Corvette for production racing (only five were ever constructed) and Ferrari failed to cheat the system with the 250 LM, which never gained homologation as a GT car either, and was therefore forced to run as a prototype. All this left the 289 Cobra freer than expected to notch up additional local and national victories around the world, as well as support Shelby-Ford's successful campaign to win the GT class of the 1965 World Sports Car Championship.

AC 289

Apart from employing such home-grown parts as Lucas electrical ancillaries, the 582 leaf spring Cobras sold by AC in Britain and Europe were basically the same as the Shelby cars. The ensuing AC 289 was, however, unique to the Thames Ditton factory and basically a coil spring chassis powered by the 289 Windsor engine. Only 27 were made, but it is thought by some aficionados to be the nicest driving, finest handling of the entire breed. What the model certainly did represent, was a final chance for AC to put its own logo on what was a Cobra in all but name – something Shelby agreed to do for all examples of the model, but reneged on very early in the project.

- A very nice example of the AC 289, complete with the perfect registration plate. Only 27 were made and some believe this model to be the sweetest driving of all the Cobra family. *Trevor Legate*

- Some 10 'Dragonsnake' drag-race Cobras were built, including two works cars, of which CSX2357 (seen here) was one. They proved very successful, adding another string to the Cobra's racing bow. *Private collection*

A few Cobra curiosities

family car these days. Still available, however, is *Carroll Shelby's Original Texas Brand Chili Mix.* The seasoning kit grew out of the first ever chili cook-off he co-organised at Terlingua back in 1967 – something that became an annual event and now regularly draws 10,000 people to the former mining town.

Quite a coup(e)

The last time one of the six Shelby Daytona Cobra Coupes came to market was in 2009 when chassis CSX2601 sold at auction for $7.25 million – a big sum then, though there is no doubt such a figure would be dwarfed if one was offered today.

The value stems from a mix of rarity and provenance, the GT class win in the 1965 World Sports Car Championship remaining a landmark moment in American motor sport history. Such pedigree has since resulted in several awards for the sister car CSX2287, which in 2014 was selected by the public to be Car of the Year in the International Historic Motoring Awards. It also became the first vehicle to be logged by the United States' Historic Vehicle Association's National Historic Vehicle Register and the first car ever to be recorded under the US Secretary of the Interior's Standards for Heritage Documentation.

Hey Little Cobra

Annette Kleinbard was the lead singer on the Teddy Bears' hit '*To Know Him is to Love Him*', but by the time she rocked up at Shelby American looking for someone to repair the bodywork of the AC Ace-Bristol she had accidentally modified, she had changed her name to Carol Connors. A by-product of her visit was the song she then penned at Shelby's suggestion called *Hey Little Cobra*, which was recorded by The Rip Chords and spent 14 weeks in the American charts of 1963, peaking at No.4, for which the lady reputedly received a Cobra of her own.

Chili con Shelby

Carroll Shelby lent his name to a variety of products over the years including *Pit Stop – A Real Man's Deodorant*, a can of which is probably worth the price of small

- Musician Carol Connors originally visited SAI to get a friend's car repaired, but ended up penning a song about the Cobra that not only became a major hit, but reputedly netted her a 289 of her own.
Private collection

Chapter 8
The Shelby legacies

The Cobra story that burst into being in 1962 around the subjects of this book – chassis CSX2000, CSX2001 and CSX2002 – continued into 1967, by which time the automotive landscape on both road and track had moved on apace. So, no doubt heavy of heart, Carroll Shelby pulled the plug on the car with which he had realised his dream. It created many highs during its five years of production, but the sweetest of all was surely achieving its maker's long-standing aim of 'kicking Ferrari's ass' and winning Class III of the 1965 World Sports Car Championship.

By the time he had gone on to mastermind Ford's inaugural Le Mans victory with the GT40, he had notched up the arguably unique treble of winning at Le Mans as a driver (1959), constructor (1964) and team manager (1966) – a pretty impressive achievement for a small town Texan, born nearly 5,000 miles from the location of the world's premier sports car race.

However, the Cobra itself is surely the greatest of his many legacies for, far from ending with the cessation of production in 1967, the phenomenon is alive and extremely well 50 years later. The majority of the 996 examples produced in period still exist and continue to be raced and displayed the world over for all to enjoy, while replicas excite a new generation of enthusiasts – whether they be examples of the many independently produced kits or the fully sanctioned evocations these days offered by Shelby American itself.

As we noted at the outset, the timing of Carroll Shelby's approach to AC Cars and Ford Motor Company could hardly have been better – the Cobra was a, some would say *the* car of its time. And following five decades of automotive evolution you could argue it is once again – now as the perfect antithesis to the oh-so-perfect but often soulless cars of today.

Some supercars in track mode can be drifted tail out, but how many elicit the raw feel of a software-free Cobra, and will the sound of an electric car ever get the heart pounding in the way a V8 Cobra is guaranteed to do? We think not.

We enthusiasts are extremely fortunate that the trio of cars on which the Cobra dynasty was built have not only survived but dwell in the best possible hands, as all three are of ever-increasing historical importance.

Who better than Dan Gurney to summarise the Cobra project and its creator:

'Brilliant name, brilliant timing! When I first saw the Shelby Cobra at Riverside Raceway in the spring of 1963, it looked almost laughable. Here was a British sports car with pre-World War II design features that had received a California hot-rod makeover: outsized Indy car Halibrand wheels, big brakes, a 289 Ford engine with Italian Weber carburettors, made a unique roadster, a belching, bucking, vibrating brute of a machine.

'Its creator Carroll Shelby, visionary and superior salesman, sold Ford Motor Company on the idea that the Cobra could beat the Corvette. And it did!

'Racing it on the mountain roads of the Targa Florio in Sicily was like riding a bull: "Ride 'em Cowboy"! The car was uncomfortable, austere and loud but once you tamed the beast it delivered the most outstanding lap times.

'The Cobra acquired an enormous fan base, inspired songs and made lasting history. It was naughty, like its creator.'

One of Shelby's attributes was surrounding himself with the right people. With Dan Gurney he had access to one of the finest drivers America has ever produced. *LAT Images*

Acknowledgements

The author is greatly indebted to the following for their assistance in the research and publication of this book: AC Owners' Club (Robin Stainer), Bernard Afchain, Hervé Arnone-Demoy, John Atkins, Anna Batho, Scott Black, Peter Brock, Marilyn Bruce, Robert Charbonneau, François Granet, Dan Gurney, Geoff Howard, Goodman Derrick LLP (Martin Emmison), Lukas Hüni, Tom Kenney, Trevor Legate, Bruce Meyer, David and Richard Milo, North Devon Metalcraft (Paul and John Evans), Wilfrid Ouellet, Porter Publishing (Ray Hutton) and RM Sotheby's (Amy Christie).

Index

Abarth Simca 70, 71, 72
AC
    289 19, 42, 43, 122
    428 19
A98 Coupe 67
Ace 10, 12, 13, 19, 24, 30, 34, 38, 41, 46, 49, 51, 62, 66, 123
AC Cars 10, 18-19, 24, 26, 31, 34, 36, 42, 45, 46, 48, 62, 66, 67, 80, 121, 122, 124
Afchain, Bernard 74, 75, 76, 77, 78
All American Racers 27, 98
Allard 45
    J2X 10, 21
Alpine 68, 72
Amiot, Marius 104
Arnone-Demoy, Hervé 73, 74, 75, 77, 78
Aston Martin 10, 17, 21, 116
    DBR1 22
Austin-Healey 21
    100S 21
    3000 73

Ballot-Léna, Claude 70
Bandini, Lorenzo 101
Barone, René 72
Behra, Jean 79, 94
Beltoise, Jean-Pierre 72
Berger, Georges 70
Bianchi, Lucien 70
Bolton, Peter 67, 80
Bondurant, Bob 67, 70, 90, 116
Bonnier, Jo 70, 79
Borel, Denis 72
Brabham 98, 102
Bridgehampton 500km 98
Brock, Peter 31, 32-33, 36, 43, 119, 120
Budapest-Prague rally 76

Camoradi team 65, 79
Canadian Track & Traffic 103
Carroll Shelby Foundation 50
Carroll Shelby School of Racing 16, 22
Carroll Shelby Trust 50, 51
Casner, Lloyd 'Lucky' 65, 66, 67, 70, 79
Cevert, François 102
Chardonnet, André 67
Chevrolet 9, 45, 90, 93, 100, 120
    Corvette 10, 14, 20, 30, 32, 39, 73, 89, 90, 93, 94, 97, 100, 102, 103, 104, 120, 121, 122, 124
    Corvette C6R 77
    Corvette Grand Sport 39, 120, 122

Christy, John 49
Cobra, Dragonsnake 51, 122
Comstock Racing 89, 96, 99, 101, 102, 103, 104
Connellsville 62, 64, 65
Cooper 30, 36, 100
Cooper-Climax 32, 79
Course de Côte d'Hébécrevon 71, 72
Course de Côte des Andelys 62, 72
Course de Côte de La Pommeraye 70, 72, 73

Daigh, Chuck 94
Daytona
    3 Hours 30, 92, 94, 95, 96, 98
    Continental 2,000km 118, 119
Duncan, Dale 21
Dupeyron, Maurice 67, 70

Ecurie Francorchamps 70
Ellenreider, Dominik 75, 76, 77
European Cars Inc. 9, 13, 61, 62, 66, 80
Everly, John 90

Faget, Gerard 70
Ferrari 10, 12, 17, 20, 24, 31, 68, 80 116, 122, 124
    166 Barchetta 18, 38
    250 GTO 67, 70, 72, 90, 93, 116, 120
    250 GT SWB 14, 77
    250 LM 39, 70, 80, 120, 122
    250 P 101
    330 P 70
    340 Mexico 21
Ferrari, Enzo 120
Fiat Abarth 70
    700 66
Ford
    Fairlane 10, 39
    Falcon, 39
    Galaxie 70
    GT40 22, 23, 27, 33, 98, 102, 103, 104, 124
    GT40 MkII 51
    GT40 MkIV 51
    Mustang 17, 32
    Zephyr MkII 10
Ford France 70, 75
Ford Motor Company 9, 10, 13, 17, 19, 22, 23, 24, 27, 29, 34, 38, 39, 40, 41, 42, 80, 116, 121, 124
Ford, Henry II 17
Forlong, Duncan 12
Formula One (F1) 21, 36, 72, 79, 94, 102,
Foyt, AJ 98

Garage de Lorraine 67, 68
Gardner, Frank 101
General Motors 10, 32, 40, 41, 94, 104, 120, 122
Giorgi, Jean-Michel 72
Goodwood 98
    Glover Trophy 79
    Revival 33, 119
Grand Prix 72, 98
    Canadian 99, 101, 102
    Italian 21
Grandsire, Henri 72
Gransart, Patrice 72
Gregory, Masten 21, 79, 80
Gurney, Dan 9, 27, 41, 79, 89, 92, 94, 95, 96, 98, 124

Hallyday, Johnny 61, 72, 74
Healey 10, 45
Hill, Graham 70, 101
Hill, Phil 21, 96
Holman & Moody 27, 93
Hooper, Doug 90
Hot Rod magazine 100
Howard, Geoff 89, 105, 106
Hudson, Skip 92
Hugus, Ed 13, 61, 62, 66, 72, 80
Hulme, Denny 51
Hüni, Lukas 76, 78

Iso Bizzarrini A3/C 77

Jaguar 49, 70
    C-type 21
    D-type 90, 94
    E-type 24, 38, 41, 49
    Mk X 38, 41
Jeffords, Jim 79
Jopp, Peter 80

Krause, Bill 9, 89, 90, 92, 93, 94, 100, 105

Lafleur, Guy 105
Lagier, Bernard 71
Lancia 68
Landereau, Pierre 72, 73, 74, 77
Le Mans
    24 Hours 10, 13, 17, 19, 21, 22, 23, 30, 31, 51, 52, 61, 65, 66, 67, 68, 77, 78, 79, 80, 98, 116, 124
    Test Weekend/Trial 9, 65, 66, 78, 79
Ligier, Guy 70
Lotus 71
    19 94
    23B 101
    49 102
    Elan 70
Lotus-Ford F3 72, 102

MacDonald, Dave 89, 9, 90, 92, 93, 94, 96, 97, 99, 118, 120
Maranello Concessionaires 70
Maserati 21, 22
    250F 21
    'Birdcage' 23, 79, 90, 94
    Tipo 151 79
McClure, George 12
McCluskey, Mike 76
McLean, Bob 103, 104
Meyer, Bruce 61, 76, 77, 78
MGA 73
Miles, Ken 9, 23, 30, 39, 41, 42, 51, 89, 90, 93, 96, 99, 101, 102, 118, 119, 120, 121
Mille Miglia 68
Miller, Greg 51, 52
Miller, Larry 51, 52, 105, 106
Milo, David 62, 65
Milo, Richard 12, 62, 65
Milo, Richard Junior 62, 65
MIRA 46
Monte Carlo Rally 18, 68
Montlhéry 66, 67, 68, 70, 71, 72, 74
    1000km de Paris 70, 71
    Coupe de Paris 68, 70
    Coupes de l'USA 66, 67, 68
Mont-Tremblant 101, 103, 104, 105
Moon, Dean 12, 14, 20, 29, 48, 49, 62
Morrogh, Henry 70
Mortemart, Baron Jean de, 66, 67, 70, 71, 75
Mosport 99, 101, 103
Moss, Stirling 61, 67, 79, 94
Myers, Rob 50

Nassau Speed Week 90, 120, 121
    Governor's Trophy race 90
    Tourist Trophy 90
Neerpasch, Jochen 67, 70
New York Auto Show 49, 50
Norma M20FC 70
North American Racing Team (NART) 80
Nürburgring 1,000km 79

OSCA MT4 21
Ostiguy, Jean Paul 103
Ouellet, Jean 9, 101, 103, 104, 105

Paris-Dakar Rally 72
Pebble Beach Concours d'Elegance 9, 50
Pibaro, André 73
Porsche 68, 79
    356 70
    550RS 73
    904 70
    904 Carrera GTS 72
    910 77
    935 K3 77
Portwine, John 18

Quail, The, Monterey 78

Rallye de l'AGACI 70, 72, 73, 75
Rathgeb, Charles 'Chuck' Jnr 96
Reims 68, 70, 72, 73, 98
Reinhart, Paul 97
Remington, Phil 27, 29, 30, 41, 90
Rétromobile 76, 78
Revillon, René-Louis 72
Rimouski Racing Team 101, 103, 104
Rindt, Jochen 80
Riverside Raceway 9, 16, 23, 30, 34, 42, 49, 50, 79, 89, 90, 92, 94, 98, 100, 105, 118, 119, 124
Rives, Johnny 72
Road & Track 49, 51
Roberts, Glenn 'Fireball' 96
Rodriguez, Pedro 101
Ruata, Franck 70, 72, 73

Said, Bob 21
Saint-Auban, Bernard de 70
Salut les Copains 72
Salvadori, Roy 10, 21, 22
Samson, André 103
Sanderson, Ninian 80
Scheckter, Jody 102
Schlesser, Jo 72, 75, 116
Sebring 12 Hours 12, 30, 51, 62, 89, 93, 97, 98, 100, 102, 103, 104, 105, 106
Shelby American 17, 23, 24, 27, 30, 32, 36, 38, 39, 40, 42, 43, 70, 80, 90, 93, 95, 96, 98, 100, 101, 106, 116, 120, 123
Shelby
    427 121
    Cobra 'Flip-Top' 30, 118, 120
    Daytona Cobra Coupe 32, 51, 52, 67, 70, 98, 100, 105, 116, 120, 123
    Mustang GT350 22, 30, 39, 102
Shelby, Aaron 50, 52
Shelby, Carroll 9, 10, 12-16, 17, 19, 20-23, 24, 27, 30, 31, 32, 34, 38, 39, 45, 46, 48, 49, 50, 51, 52, 61, 62, 77, 79, 80, 90, 92, 93, 94, 97, 100, 106, 115, 116, 119, 121, 122, 123, 124-125
Shoen, Michael 105, 106
Simon, André 67, 70
Spencer, Lew 96
Sports Car Club of America (SCCA) 21, 30, 65, 93, 94, 96, 97, 116
Sports Car Graphic 49, 50
Sports Illustrated 21
Standard-Triumph 68
Sunbeam Alpine 99, 102
Surtees, John 101

Targa Florio 98
Thompson, Mickey 90, 94, 100
Tojeiro, John 18, 19, 36, 38, 42
Tomaso, Alejandro de 12
Tour de France Automobile 9, 14, 61, 66, 67, 68, 70, 78
Tremblay, Michel 105
Trintignant, Maurice 70

Vincent, Jean Marie 61, 62, 65, 66, 67, 68, 70, 71, 72, 73, 75, 76, 77, 78, 79
Watkins Glen 65, 99
Wietzes, Eppie 9, 99, 101, 102, 104
Wietzes, Jan 99
Wyer, John 10, 17, 21

Zurini, Emmanuel 72